# The Selected Poems of Sir John Davies

# The Selected Poems of Sir John Davies

*Edited with an introduction by Dr. Joe Carlson*

ROMAN ROADS CLASSICS

**Also in the Roman Roads Classics series:**

*Inferno: Book One of the Divine Comedy*, by Dante Alighieri, translated by Joe Carlson

*Purgatorio: Book Two of the Divine Comedy*, by Dante Alighieri, translated by Joe Carlson

*Paradiso: Book Three of the Divine Comedy*, by Dante Alighieri, translated by Joe Carlson

*The Iliad*, by Homer, a new rendering by Wesley Callihan

*The Odyssey*, by Homer, a new rendering by Wesley Callihan

*On Duties*, by Cicero, translated by Walter Miller, introduction by Wesley Callihan

*Paradise Lost & Paradise Regained* by John Milton, introduction by Joe Carlson

---

The Selected Poems of Sir John Davies, by Sir John Davies
Edited with an introduction by Dr. Joe Carlson

Copyright © 2025 by Roman Roads Press
Published by Roman Roads Press,
Moscow, Idaho
RomanRoadsPress.com / permissions: info@romanroadspress.com

General Editor: Dr. Joe Carlson
Introduction: Dr. Joe Carlson
Editor: Carissa Hale
Cover Design and Interior Layout: Carissa Hale

The Selected Poems of Sir John Davies, by Sir John Davies

Roman Roads Press / Roman Roads Classics

ISBN: 978-1-963505-18-4
Version 1.0.1 • September 2025

# CONTENTS

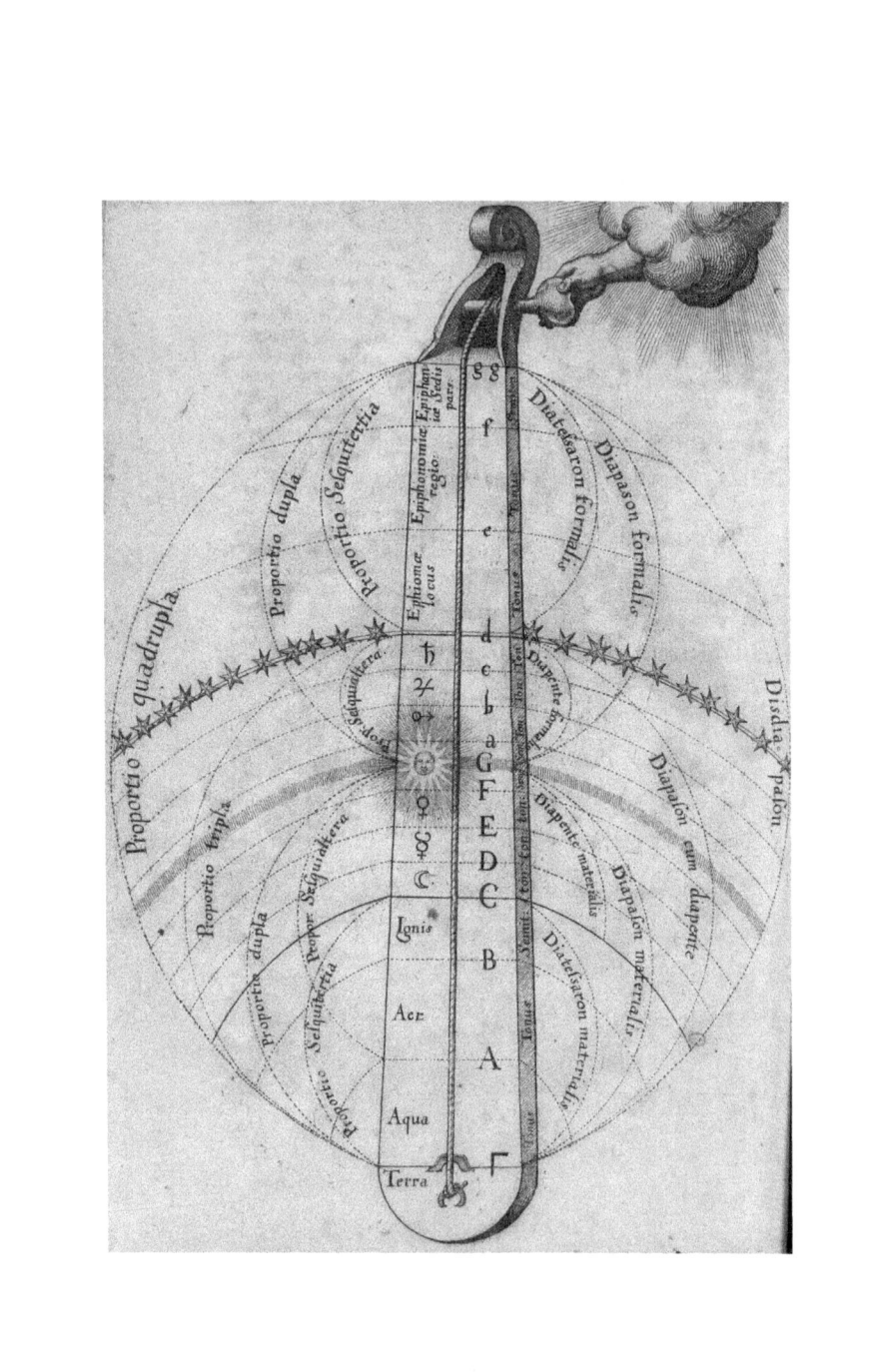

# AN EXPLANATION OF THE COVER IMAGE

The cover image perhaps needs an explanation. In 1617, illustrator and Christian mystic Robert Fludd published his controversial *A Metaphysical, Physical, and Technical History of Both the Greater and the Lesser World, divided into two volumes according to the difference of the cosmos.* In that work among many other things, Fludd argues for a congruency between the Cosmos Major (the universe, or macrocosm) and the Cosmos Minor (the human being, or microcosm). This late Renaissance theory (expanding on Medieval themes and doctrines) explores the relationship of the two realms and how they mirror each other in some way. The cover image is taken from this book and represents the Mundane Monochord (*monochordum mundanum*). The monochord was an ancient, single stringed instrument on which the relationship of the different musical intervals (fourth, fifth, octave, etc.) was easily demonstrated. Fludd uses that image here to illustrate his theory that the entire cosmos functions as a monochord, with God as the "divine player." The caption to the image reads: "Here, moreover, we have composed the mundane monochord with its proportions, consonances, and intervals exactly; whose mover we have depicted in this way as being outside the world." This image becomes a symbol of what many theologians have called "cosmic harmony" related to the "music (harmony) of the spheres," a model of the universe that goes back to Boethius and beyond. According to this model, and consistent with Davies' own depiction of the world in his poem *Orchestra*, the world is made of music (or dance). The cosmos is the song of God, sung through the Word, upheld by the power of His voice. He keeps the world "in tune" as it were, as the image represents, and the spheres of heaven dance to the music of the Empyrean (the spiritual heaven that surrounds the entire material cosmos). Furthermore, the image represents the cosmic harmony and unity that is reflected in the microcosm that is the human being. Thus, just as the universe is made of music that exists in harmony with itself, tuned by the hand of God, so too are we. The harmony of the spheres and their celestial governors (angelic beings), is reflected, or mirrored, in the harmony of the body and soul. For more information on this model of the cosmos, one should read Dante's *Divine Comedy* and Pseudo-Dionysius' *Celestial Hierarchies*.

# A SHORT BIOGRAPHY OF SIR JOHN DAVIES

John Davies was born in Wiltshire, England in 1569, five years after William Shakespeare and seventeen years after Edmund Spenser. His father, a tanner, died when he was very young, leaving him and his two older brothers to be raised by their mother. He was educated first at Winchester College and then at Queen's College in Oxford before enrolling at the Middle Temple in London (one of four houses, or Inns of Court, in which barristers were trained) in 1588. He received his bachelor of arts in 1590, and was called to the bar in 1595. He was disbarred three years later for breaking a cudgel over the head of his former friend, Richard Martin (to whom his poem *Orchestra* is dedicated). In 1601, after making a public apology to Martin, he was readmitted to the Temple society. Two years later, he was appointed by King James to be the Solicitor-General for Ireland, and then Attorney-General in 1606. A staunch protestant, Davies' chief goal was to eradicate Roman Catholicism from the island by banishing the priests, an effort which received much support from England. During this time, Davies was intimately involved in the planning and implementation of the Plantation of Ulster, a colonizing project in which the inhabitants of rural North Ireland were required to speak English, become Protestant, and pledge their allegiance to the English crown. This became a model for future colonization efforts, most notably in North America. The mixed success of this project in Ulster led to Davies' famous treatise, "A Discovery of the True Causes why Ireland was never entirely Subdued, nor brought under Obedience of the Crown of England, until the Beginning of his Majesty's Happy Reign," which was published in 1612. In 1614, he was elected as Speaker of the House of Commons in Ireland, a position he held until his return to England in 1619, where he served occasionally as a circuit judge in the English courts. An avid supporter of King Charles, Davies was appointed Chief Justice in November, 1626, though he did not live to take office. He died of apoplexy less than a month later on the 8th of December. He was buried at St. Martin-in-the-Fields in London, and it is said that John Donne preached the funeral oration.

Throughout his tenure as a barrister, Davies also wrote poetry. *Orchestra, or, A Poeme of Dancing*, was published in 1594, with *Nosce Teipsum* coming out in 1599. Davies quickly became a favorite of Queen Elizabeth, leading to the release of the *Hymnes of Astraea*, a long series of acrostic poems, each based on the phrase *Elisabetha Regina*. Additionally, he wrote dozens of epigrams, sonnets, and other miscellaneous poems, including many metrical versions of the Psalms. He is the master poet almost no one has heard of. Poet and scholar Malcolm Guite comments on Davies' relative obscurity compared to his more celebrated contemporaries:

> Sir John Davies is due for a revival. He is an underrated poet not because he is neglected or forgotten, but because he is remembered for the wrong reasons and in the wrong context. He has been pressed into service as a continuous supplier and illustrator of background. He lives in other people's footnotes. From the time he was used to provide a kind of photographer's back-drop to the works of Shakespeare in E.M.W. Tillyard's excellent book *The Elizabethan World Picture*, he has been quarried for example and illustration of the cultural background of the Elizabethan age. Relegating Davies to survive as a kind of two-dimensional academic wallpaper, decorating the rooms in which other poets are allowed to live and move and have their being in three dimensions, has done him no service, other than preserving his name and fragments of his verse torn out of context.[1]

---

1   Malcom Guite, *Faith, Hope and Poetry: Theology and the Poetic Imagination* (London: Routledge, 2016), 75.

x

The following volume is an answer to the call to revive the poetry of Sir John Davies. Though his output, counted in page numbers, is not as significant as either Shakespeare or Spenser, his quality of thought and argument, his poetic, philosophic, and theological intuition, and his facility with the English language firmly establish him in the pantheon of great Elizabethan poets. He should be recognized as such.

# INTRODUCTION

*by Dr. Joe Carlson*

We are currently living in the make-believe world of Nothing-Buttery. Far from being a comment on food preferences, Nothing-Buttery refers to the kind of scientific reductionism that tells us we are "nothing but...," and then fills in the blank with whatever current trend is floating about. This is nothing new. The Pre-Socratic philosophers engaged in Nothing-Buttery when they said the cosmos is ultimately *nothing but* fire (Heraclitus), *nothing but* water and air (Thales), *nothing but* numbers (Pythagoras). Perhaps this is an oversimplification of their various philosophies, but you get the idea. Later philosophers, such as Democritus, Epicurus, and Lucretius, believed we were *nothing but* a collection of atoms. Down through the ages, men have tried to reduce our existence to *nothing but*: *nothing but* sense perception (Hume), or *nothing but* the grandchildren of monkeys (Darwin), or *nothing but* sacks of protoplasm existing at relatively stable temperatures (modern science). It is this most recent "nothing but" that has taken such deep root in our culture today. Modern science, downstream from Darwin and Hume, refuses to acknowledge anything supernatural about our existence. Existence is the byproduct of time and chance acting on matter; naturalistic and materialistic causes are the only explanations given any consideration. No matter how crazy or insane they may sound to rational minds ("The universe evolved from a single cell? Really? C'mon..."), they are the only answers allowed by the governing intelligentsia. We are *nothing but* what modern scientific journals say we are, which, as it turns out, is nothing much.

Into this blind, chaotic world, the poetry of Sir John Davies shines like the piercing rays of a lighthouse, firmly grounded on a rock that is higher than us. Castaways on a turbulent sea, blown by tempestuous winds, the stars above us obscured by giant thunderheads of fear and doubt, we are in need of such a light, guiding us to safety. Our chosen ship, the *Nothing-Buttery*, was plagued from the start, its hull full of holes, its mast as sturdy as a blade of grass, its sails as thin as tissue paper. But in our blindness, in our willful rejection of the cosmos we actually inhabit, not to mention its very real Maker, we took to our ship as if she were the most seaworthy of crafts. Many voices warned us of the troubles ahead. But our destination, the fabled land of Existential Autonomy and its capital city of Expressive Individualism, where everyone was free to do and be whatever one wanted, regardless of the constraints of nature, was too great a draw to let us hear wisdom. And so here we are, shipwrecked on the sea of reality, our only hope being the return journey. But who will guide us?

Indeed, our only hope is in the One who "made the heaven, and earth, the sea and all that therein is" (Psalm 146:6). We will, all of us and without exception, one day be confronted with the reality of Him who sits on the throne. Every knee will bow. Every tongue will confess. But before the great and terrible day of the Lord comes, He kindly and graciously uses means, leading us back to Himself a step at a time. And the means always suit the particular blindness in question. One such means, perfectly suited to the insanity of the current reign of Nothing-Buttery, is the collection of poems you now hold in your hand.

The reduction of all things to naturalistic causes gives men and women the false security and apparent freedom to define their own existence according to their own whims. But what this fails to account for is the inescapable feeling that we were made (*made*, mind you) for something more. The scientific method is a wonderful tool for describing with accuracy the careful observation of certain phenomena; it cannot tell you why you exist. The great tragedy of reducing everything to naturalistic causes is that it bars from serious public discourse the asking of humanity's most fundamental and persistent questions: Who am I? What am I? What happens when I die? Do I have a soul? What is consciousness?

What is truth? Why is there evil in the world? Is beauty really in the eye of the beholder, or is it more than that? Who and where is God? Is He even real?

If you have asked yourself any of those questions and still have not found a compelling answer, then you probably have not read the Bible. You have probably not read any quality poetry, either. Science can speak with a great deal of precision about what we can perceive. Poetry tells us about what lies beneath, within, and beyond what we perceive. But what is it that we perceive? How do we perceive it? How does that work, exactly? Poetry allows us to understand not just *what* we know, but *how* we know as well.

What do I mean? Light, traveling from the sun, lands on a certain object, reflecting certain colors and shapes. That reflection rides certain waves and eventually lands in our eyes. But is that knowledge? Let's say the object the light originally hit was a tree. Is the action of our eyes receiving the light bouncing off the tree the reason we know it is a tree? In other words, is our knowledge of the treeness of that particular object merely a mechanical reaction to receiving the incoming waves of light? Some synapse is triggered in our brain, and we, conditioned by experience and social convention, know we have seen a tree: is that how it works? Or is there something in us, something like a soul or mind or imagination, that reaches out to what our eyes have gathered, and truly perceives the image in all its polysemous glory? Is there a light in our own soul (or mind or imagination), the source of which is not in us, that from within shines on the object gathered by our eyes and is able to find meaning in what it sees? The poet Sir John Davies argued for the latter option. But what does that mean and why is it important? In the world of Nothing-Buttery, we can only explain knowledge and understanding in terms of mechanistic processes: photons hitting retinas, optic nerves sending signals to the brain. There is no soul that you can point to in your body, no mind that can be found among all your organs. But if you take this route, you have to admit that there is no meaning either. The random assortment of particles that we happen to call light bounce off the random assortment of particles we happen to call a tree and hit the random assortment of particles we happen to call our eyes. And because that event has happened more than once, we grow comfortable naming certain random assortments, as if that gave them meaning. But it doesn't. It's only a name tag. In the world of Nothing-Buttery, name tags are simply handles to avoid confusion. They do not explain what the thing is, or why it is, or what it means. Deep down, we know this materialistic reductionism is complete bunk, and so we sneak in through the back door the ideas of consciousness, meaning, morality, purpose, and beauty. As a matter of fact, we sneak in the idea of *ideas* themselves. For what existence in the natural world does an idea have? Next time you have one, point to it. Try and grab hold of it and pin it down. You can't do it, for ideas belong to the spiritual world, the world of invisibilities, the world only explained by the Bible... and poetry.

Why do I keep coming back to poetry? Because this is a book of poems and not a book of theology, though the two often go together, as you will see. Poetry, as noted already, speaks to the reality behind the phenomena, above and beyond the events explained by science. In his essay, "Bluspels and Flalansferes: A Semantic Nightmare," C. S. Lewis discusses the difference between reason/truth (science) and imagination/meaning (poetry):

> It will have escaped no one that in such a scale of writers the poets will take the highest place; and among the poets those who have at once the tenderest care for old words and the surest instinct for the creation of new metaphors. But it must not be supposed that I am in any sense putting forward the imagination as the organ of truth. We are not talking of truth, but of meaning: meaning which is the antecedent condition both of truth and falsehood, whose antithesis is not error but nonsense. I am a rationalist. For me, reason is the natural organ of truth; but imagination is the organ of meaning. Imagination, producing new metaphors or revivifying old, is not the cause of truth, but its condition.[2]

---

2  C. S. Lewis, "Bluspels and Flalansferes: A Semantic Nightmare" from *Selected Literary Essays*, ed. Walter Hooper (Cambridge, UK: Cambridge University Press, 2019), 265.

In other words, the imagination is where we discover what words mean; only after we understand their meaning can we decide whether something is true or not. That final judgement call is the duty of reason; establishing the meaning beforehand is the function of the imagination. This is why poetry is so important, and why Lewis accords poets the highest place among writers. Metaphor and image are their natural habitat, the currency in which they trade, the very air they breathe. And it is by metaphor, by the natural association of different ideas and words and objects, that we understand the nature of reality. More on that in a moment.

Put another way, poetry demonstrates for us what the imagination is and does, that image-laden landscape of our soul where the meaning of words are apprehended. There is a light (one of Davies' most beloved metaphors) in each of us that shines outward onto reality, the light of perception and understanding. As the imagination gathers data by means of the senses, it actively organizes and sorts the images it receives within the landscape of our soul, shaping our consciousness according to the reality we behold and participate in. (This shaping, by the way, happens both in our interactions with the world and with the world as imitated and represented in literature.) But where does that inner light come from?[3]

We have a hard time answering that question, because we don't even think to ask it in the first place. As Davies says in *Nosce Teipsum* (*Know Thyself*):

> All things without, which round about we see,
> We seek to know, and how therewith to do;
> But that whereby we *reason*, *live* and *be*,
> Within ourselves, we strangers are thereto.
>
> We seek to know the moving of each sphere,
> And the strange cause of th' ebbs and floods of *Nile*;
> But of that clock within our breasts we bear,
> The subtle motions we forget the while.

---

3   In what follows, I am indebted to Malcolm Guite's insightful reading of Davies' poetry, found in the third chapter of his fantastic *Faith, Hope, and Poetry: Theology and the Poetic Imagination* (publication details listed at the end of the Introduction). For the student who wants to go deeper, I cannot recommend Guite's book highly enough.

We that acquaint ourselves with every *Zone*
And pass both *Tropics* and behold the *Poles*,
When we come home, are to ourselves unknown,
And unacquainted still with our own *Souls*.

We study *Speech* but others we persuade;
We *leech-craft* learn, but others cure with it;
We interpret *laws*, which other men have made,
But read not those which in our hearts are writ.
~ Lines 89–104

Why? Why do we refuse to obey the ancient dictum, "Know Thyself"? John Calvin, the great reformer, writing just a few decades before Davies, recognized that a true knowledge of God depends on a true knowledge of self, and that a true knowledge of self likewise depends on a true knowledge of God. Could it be that we rest in our uneasy ignorance of self because it allows us to stay ignorant of God as well? While that may provide momentary comfort, as do all illusions and lies, it cannot be the foundation of a functioning epistemology (how we know what we know), something every single person needs. This willful blindness has a very simple name: sin. And in our sin, we refuse to acknowledge that's what it is. Davies continues:

Is it because the mind is like the eye,
Through which it gathers knowledge by degrees—
Whose rays reflect not, but spread outwardly:
Not seeing itself when other things it sees?

No, doubtless; for the mind can backward cast
Upon herself, her understanding light;
But she is so corrupt, and so defaced,
As her own image doth herself affright

[…]

Even so *Man's Soul* which did God's image bear,
And was at first fair, good, and spotless pure;
Since with her *sins* her beauties blotted were,
Doth of all sights her own sight least endure:

For even at first reflection she espies,
Such strange *chimeras*, and such monsters there;
Such toys, such *antics*, and such vanities,
As she retires, and shrinks for shame and fear.

And as the man loves least at home to be,
That hath a sluttish house haunted with *spirits*;
So she, impatient her own faults to see,
Turns from herself and in strange things delights.
                    ~ Lines 105–112, 121–132

In our sin, we refuse to look ourselves square in the eye with honesty. Impatient with our own faults, we turn from our true nature, and take delight in "strange things." What are we to do? How can we, stuck in the willful blindness of our sin, ever hope to truly know ourselves, and thus God, and thus the meaning and purpose of the entire cosmos? Davies gives us the answer:

That *Power* which gave me eyes the World to view,
To see myself infused an *inward light*;
Whereby my *Soul*, as by a mirror true,
Of her own form may take a perfect sight.

But as the sharpest eye discerneth nought,
Except the *sun*-beams in the air do shine;
So the best *Soul* with her reflecting thought,
Sees not herself without some light divine.

*O Light* which mak'st the light, which makes the day!
Which set'st the eye without, and mind within;
Lighten my spirit with one clear heavenly ray,
Which now to view itself doth first begin.
                    ~ Lines 193–204

Put simply, we need Christ, who "mak'st the light, which makes the day," the Light of the World, the light in which we see light, the light who shines in the darkness, the light that is our life, the true light that gives light to everyone. Only by the light of Christ, lightening "my spirit with one clear heavenly ray" can I begin to truly see myself. Without the light of Christ, our souls can see about as far as our eyes in a pitch black cave. But with the light of Christ, our souls can see, *truly see*, the images our eyes take in, with real knowledge and understanding. And because this is true, the reverse is true as well: the fact that we can see and understand the images our eyes take in, with real knowledge and understanding, means that we all to some extent have as the foundation of our soul, the light of Christ, what John calls "the light of men" (John 1:4). No one made in the image of God can completely turn off that light. We can dim and obscure it by sin, but that basic light in us is our consciousness, our rational faculty. In other words, the only reason we can know anything is because the "light of men" shines in our hearts. Not in the sense that we are redeemed and saved from our sins, but that we can actually see and understand the world around us. Thus, even the pagan imagination can communicate meaning we recognize as being fundamentally true. For their imaginations are kindled by a spark that comes not from them, but from the One in whom they have their being, the One in whose image they are made.

As bearers of the *imago Dei*, we each have the light of understanding. Again, sin dims and obscures that light, confusing our understanding both of ourselves and of the world, leading to the irrationality of Nothing-Buttery. But human reason, however obscured by our sin, still has its source not in ourselves but in the One Who breathed within us the breath of life. Again, this is why those who hate God and reject Jesus can still recognize and know plenty that is true about this world: two and two is four, things of a certain weight fall to the ground when dropped, hydrogen and oxygen, in the proper amounts, make water. That knowledge is only possible because the "light of men" shines in their hearts, giving them rationality and a certain degree of common-grace understanding. However, when we come to Christ in faith, submitting ourselves to Him, the scales come off and we see our dependence on Him, see ourselves for who we truly are, which leads us to honor God as God and give Him thanks. Regeneration is the movement toward seeing all things rightly, in their proper order, through the proper lens of gratitude. In Him, and because we see Him first, we see the deeper, spiritual significance of all things. In Him we know that even if stars are made of gas, they cannot be reduced to nothing but gas. In Christ, our internal lamp is restored and we can say with Davies:

> I know my body's of so frail a kind,
> As force without, fevers within can kill;
> I know the heavenly nature of my mind,
> But 'tis corrupted both in wit and will:
>
> I know my *Soul* hath power to know all things,
> Yet is she blind and ignorant in all;
> I know I am one of Nature's little kings,
> Yet to the least and vilest things am thrall.
>
> I know my life's a pain and but a span,
> I know my *Sense* is mocked with every thing:
> And to conclude, I know myself a MAN,
> Which is a *proud*, and yet a *wretched* thing.
> ~ Lines 169–180

Humility, then, is the first step away from the lies of Nothing-Buttery. I have been created and am entirely dependent on God for my existence. I therefore do not have the authority (nor the individual autonomy) to define my own existence. I live in a world defined by Another, and I belong to Him. Davies' *Nosce Teipsum* gives us a working understanding of how we can know what that world is by first giving us an understanding of our own selves. Starting from a place of humility, from a recognition that all I have, all I am, all this world is, is a gift, enables us to see it truly, through the Light that lightens both it and me.

But what is the world? What is its meaning? How should we talk about it? If it is more than just a random collection of atoms functioning at a fairly stable temperature, then what is it? It is helpful to recognize that all of the words that follow the "nothing but" are, well, nothing but metaphors. Heraclitus said all is fire, but I'm not actually burning right now, nor do I see any flames nearby. And neither did Heraclitus. Lucretius loved the idea of very small atoms at the base of everything, but what we actually see and interact with is much larger, much more real to us than those tiny marbles (even if we call them neutrons and electrons, or quarks). Whatever we do, we have to use a metaphor to describe the world around us. There is simply too much diversity, too much complexity to not speak of the world metaphorically. So, choose your metaphor. But choose wisely. Whatever you say actually has to correspond to the full scope of reality.

Davies chose the word *dancing*. In his magnificent poem *Orchestra*, which was published before *Nosce Teipsum*, the poet describes the whole of the fabric of creation as a dance, each part joyfully and purposefully in motion with the whole. Have you been to a wedding where, at the reception, the bride and groom, along with the wedding party and all the guests join in a large group dance, where each individual member participates in the whole, each person integral to the motion of the body, all celebrating the happy couple and rejoicing together with them? For Davies, that is the best metaphor for the cosmos: one giant, ongoing dance, in which each participates in all, and all in each, all in celebration of the Love who set it all in motion. In the narrative of the poem, Antinous, one of the suitors wooing Penelope, patient wife of long-absent Odysseus, asks the queen to dance. She demurs, siding with what she thinks is the reticence of her forefathers to dance. Antinous argues the opposite, that dancing was part of the original fabric of civilization, recognized by their forefathers as a formal characteristic of the cosmos. He then launches into a long treatise on the nature of the world, what and why it is, in order to persuade Penelope (the "bright Lady") of the fittingness of dancing. He begins,

> Dancing (bright Lady) then began to be,
> When the first seeds whereof the world did spring
> The Fire, Air, Earth, and Water did agree,
> By Love's persuasion, Nature's mighty King,
> To learn their first disordered combating:
>> And, in a dance such measure to observe,
>> As all the world their motion should preserve.

Since when they still are carried in a round,
And changing come one in another's place,
Yet do they neither mingle nor confound,
But every one does keep the bounded space
Wherein the dance doth bid it turn or trace:
   This wondrous miracle doth Love devise
   For Dancing is Love's proper exercise.
             ~ Stanzas 17–18

The world is not a mere collection of independent atoms, or a me-
chanical clock (see stanza 115), wound up and then left alone. It is
a harmony of elements, mutually engaged with one another under
the direction of Love, "Nature's mighty King." This is not the
depersonalized love of the later Romantics; far less is this the "do-
whatever-feels-right-as-long-as-it-doesn't-hurt-anyone-else"  love
of our own fractured times. No, this is Love Himself, the God who
is Love, the Love of the Father manifested in the person of the
Son. This is Jesus, in, by, through, and for whom all things were
made, who by the word of His power, holds all things together like
a perfectly balanced wheel:

Like this, he framed the gods' eternal bower,
And of a shapeless and confusèd mass
By his through-piercing and digesting power
The turning vault of heaven formèd was:
Whose starry wheels he hath so made to pass,
   As that their movings do a music frame
   And they themselves, still dance unto the same.

Or if this All which round about we see
(As idle Morpheus some sick brains hath taught)
Of undivided motes compactèd be,
How was this goodly Architecture wrought?
Or by what means were they together brought?
   They err that say they did concur by chance,
   Love made them meet in a well-ordered dance.
             ~ Stanzas 19–20

What lies at the heart of all reality? Undivided motes, or atoms? One or all of the elements? No, the music of God rests at the foundation of all things, framed by the responding dance of the created elements, moving in harmony with and in obedience to the song of their Master. How did the world come about? By long years of evolution? By chance? No, they were brought together (*ex nihilo*) by the good Architect, the Choreographer, the Conductor, the Composer. The Word (or Song) of God, who in the beginning was with God and who was God, the one through whom all things came into being, He brought all things together "in a well-ordered dance."

It matters how you tell the story of the creation of the cosmos. It matters what you believe to lie at the foundation of everything. It matters what metaphors are shaping your imagination. Those dwelling in Nothing-Buttery beleive they have nothing but inert and random bits of matter to look to. Their lives will, therefore, be framed by chaos and filled with an empty, unfulfilled longing for the *something more* they refuse to see. But for those who look up into the heavens and hear the sweet music of the spheres, who look out and recognize the timpani of the undulating sea, the woodwinds of the forest glades, the flutes of all the birds in the air, and the triumphant brass of every sunrise, they will hear order and glimpse the eternal Beauty that satisfies every longing of the soul. For in this they will have tasted the Composer's love, Who with His music has made all the world to dance.

The poetry of Sir John Davies is the answer to a question we haven't even known to ask. But asking and answering that question is critical to regaining a proper understanding of who we are, truly, according to the fixed boundaries of Creation, and not our own delusions. We have, in these two poems of Sir John Davies, a poetry of true meaning, telling us not only who we are (*Orchestra*) but how we know as well (*Nosce Teipsum*). And the timing couldn't be better. As poet Malcolm Guite observes,

> Davies stood at the threshold of modernism and tried to foresee and forestall some of its worst excesses. We stand at the end of the modernist period, on the threshold of

post-modernism, when the consensus of the Enlightenment project is breaking up on every side. We need to return to the teaching of poets like Davies who mediate to us the insights of the pre-modern age, which speak directly to the heart of a post-modern cultural crisis.[4]

Often overshadowed by the work of his more famous contemporaries, Spenser and Shakespeare, Davies' poetry of meaning is due for a revival. His is a voice desperately needed in the midst of our current intellectual malaise. A new generation is rising, searching for answers, desperate to understand the cosmic coherence they intuitively feel. Lied to by our own modern-day poets and lyricists, it is high time we return to the voices of sanity, the poets who took seriously and believed implicitly the first words of Scripture: "In the beginning God created the heavens and the earth."

Too long out of print, we have collected in this volume not only the two major works discussed above but also over fifty metricized Psalms and a collection of miscellaneous poems that give a fuller picture of the late sixteenth-century poet. Where possible, we retained the original capitalization and italicization. However, we have modernized the spelling, making Davies' Elizabethan poetry accessible to modern audiences. This represents the first time a large collection of Davies' poems has been published in such a way.

### For Further Reading:

*The Complete Poems of Sir John Davies.* Edited by Rev. Alexander B. Grosart. London: Chatto and Windus, Picadilly, 1876.

*The Poems of Sir John Davies.* Edited by Robert Krueger. Oxford: Clarendon Press, 1975.

Guite, Malcolm. *Faith, Hope, and Poetry: Theology and the Poetic Imagination.* London: Routledge, 206.

---

4  Guite, *Faith, Hope and Poetry*, 100.

# The Selected Poems of
# Sir John Davies

# Orchestra

(1594)

or

# A Poem of Dancing

Judicially proving the true observation of time and measure, in
the Authenticall and laudable use of Dancing.

Ovid. Art. Aman. lib I

Si vox est, canta: si mollia
brachia, salta

Et quacunque potes dote
placere, place.[1]

## Dedications

*TO HIS VERY FRIEND, MA. RICH. MARTIN.*

To whom shall I this dancing Poem send,
This sudden, rash, half-capreol of my wit?
To you, first mover and sole cause of it,
Mine-own-selve's better half, my dearest friend.
O, would you yet my Muse some Honey lend
From your mellifluous tongue, whereon doth sit
*Suada* in Majesty, that I may fit
These harsh beginnings with a sweeter end.
You know the modest Sun full fifteen times
Blushing did rise, and blushing did descend,
While I in making of these ill made rhymes,
My golden hours unthriftily did spend:
Yet, if in friendship you these numbers praise,
I will misspend another fifteen days.

---

1  If [there] is a voice, sing; if [there are] soft arms, dance.
And by whatever gift you are able to please, please.
Ovid, *Art of Love* (*Ars Amatoria*) Book 1, Part 15.

## TO THE PRINCE.

Sir, whatsoever *YOU* are pleased to do
It is your special praise, that you are bent,
And sadly set your princely mind thereto:
Which makes *YOU* in each thing so excellent.
Hence is it that *YOU* came so soon to be
A man-at-arms in every point aright;
The fairest flower of noble chivalry;
And of Saint *George* his band, the bravest knight.
And hence it is, that all your youthful train
In activeness and grace, *YOU* do excel;
When *YOU* do courtly dancings entertain
Then Dancing's praise may be presented well
To *YOU*, whose action adds more praise thereto,
Then all the Muses with their pens can do.

# Orchestra

## or

# A Poem of Dancing

### 1

here lives the man that never yet did hear
Of chaste *Penelope*, *Ulysses'* Queen?
Who kept her faith unspotted twenty year
Till he returned that far away had been,
And many men, and many towns had seen:
Ten year at siege of *Troy* he lingering lay,
And ten year in the Midland-sea did stray.

### 2

*Homer*, to whom the Muses did carouse,
A great deep cup with heavenly Nectar filled,
The greatest, deepest cup in *Jove's* great house,
(For *Jove* himself had so expressly willed)
He drank of all, ne let one drop be spilled;
    Since when, his brain that had before been dry,
    Became the wellspring of all Poetry.

### 3

*Homer* doth tell in his abundant verse,
The long laborious travails of the man,
And of his Lady too he doth rehearse,
How she eludes with all the Art she can,
Th' ungrateful love which other Lords began;
    For of her Lord false Fame long since had sworn,
    That *Neptune's* Monsters had his carcass torn.

### 4

All this he tells, but one thing he forgot,
One thing, most worthy his eternal song,
But he was old, and blind, and saw it not,
Or else he thought he should *Ulysses* wrong,
To mingle it, his Tragic acts among.
    Yet was there not in all the world of things,
    A sweeter burden for his Muse's wings.

### 5

The Courtly love *Antinous* did make,
*Antinous* that fresh and jolly Knight,
Which of the gallants that did undertake
To win the Widow, had most wealth and might,
Wit to persuade, and beauty to delight.
    The Courtly love he made unto the Queen,
    *Homer* forgot as if it had not been.

### 6

Sing then *Terpsichore*,[2] my light Muse, sing
His gentle Art and cunning courtesy:
You, Lady, can remember every thing
For you are daughter of Queen Memory,
But sing a plain and easy Melody:
    For the soft mean that warbleth but the ground,
    To my rude ear doth yield the sweetest sound.

### 7

One only night's discourse I can report,
When the great Torch-bearer of heaven was gone
Down in a mask unto the *Ocean's* Court,
To revel it with *Tethys*[3] all alone;
*Antinous* disguisèd and unknown
    Like to the spring in gaudy Ornament
    Unto the Castle of the Princess went.

---

2   The muse of dance
3   Daughter of Uranus and Gaia, mother of the river gods

## 8

The sovereign Castle of the rocky Isle
Wherein *Penelope* the Princess lay,
Shone with a thousand Lamps, which did exile
The dim dark shades, and turned the night to day,
Not *Jove's* blue Tent what time the Sunny ray
    Behind the bulwark of the earth retires
    Is seen to sparkle with more twinkling fires.

## 9

That night the Queen came forth from far within,
And in the presence of her Court was seen,
For the sweet singer *Phemius* did begin
To praise the Worthies that at Troy had been;
Somewhat of her *Ulysses* she did ween
    In his grave Hymn the heav'nly man would sing,
    Or of his wars, or of his wandering.

## 10

*Pallas* that hour with her sweet breath divine
Inspired immortal beauty in her eyes,
That with celestial glory she did shine,
Brighter than *Venus* when she doth arise
Out of the waters to adorn the skies;
    The wooers all amazèd do admire,
    And check their own presumptuous desire.

## 11

Only *Antinous* when at first he viewed
Her starbright eyes that with new honor shined,
Was not dismayed, but there-with-all renewed
The noblesse and the splendor of his mind;
And as he did fit circumstances find,
    Unto the Throne he boldly 'gan advance,
    And with fair manners wooed the Queen to dance.

### 12

Goddess of women, since your heavenliness
Hath now vouchsafed itself to represent
To our dim eyes, which though they see the less
Yet are they blest in their astonishment;
Imitate heaven, whose beauties excellent
    Are in continual motion day and night,
    And move thereby more wonder and delight.

### 13

Let me the mover be, to turn about
Those glorious ornaments that Youth and Love
Have fixed in you, every part throughout,
Which if you will in timely measure move,
Not all those precious Gems in heav'n above
    Shall yield a sight more pleasing to behold,
    With all their turns and tracings manifold."

### 14

With this the modest Princess blushed and smiled,
Like to a clear and rosy eventide;
And softly did return this answer mild:
"Fair Sir; you needs must fairly be denied
Where your demand cannot be satisfied.
    My feet, which only nature taught to go,
    Did never yet the Art of footing know.

### 15

But why persuade you me to this new rage?
(For all disorder and misrule is new,)
For such misgovernment in former age
Our old divine Forefathers never knew,
Who if they lived, and did the follies view
    Which their fond Nephews make their chief affairs,
    Would hate themselves that had begot such heirs."

### 16

Sole heir of Virtue, and of Beauty both,
Whence comes it" (*Antinous* replies)
"That your imperious virtue is so loth
To grant your beauty her chief exercise?
Or from what spring does your opinion rise
 That Dancing is a frenzy and a rage,
 First known and used in this new-fangled age?

### 17

Dancing (bright Lady) then began to be,
When the first seeds whereof the world did spring
The Fire, Air, Earth, and water did agree,
By Love's persuasion, Nature's mighty King,
To leave their first disordered combating;
 And, in a dance such measure to observe,
 As all the world their motion should preserve.

### 18

Since when they still are carried in a round,
And changing come one in another's place;
Yet do they neither mingle nor confound,
But every one doth keep the bounded space
Wherein the Dance doth bid it turn or trace:
 This wondrous miracle did Love devise,
 For Dancing is Love's proper exercise.

### 19

Like this, he framed the Gods' eternal bower,
And of a shapeless and confusèd mass
By his through-piercing and digesting power
The turning vault of heaven formèd was:
Whose starry wheels he hath so made to pass,
 As that their movings do a music frame
 And they themselves still dance unto the same.

### 20

Or if this (All) which round about we see
(As idle *Morpheus* some sick brains hath taught)
Of undivided motes compactèd be,
How was this goodly Architecture wrought?
Or by what means were they together brought?
    They err that say they did concur by chance,
    Love made them meet in a well-ordered dance.

### 21

As when *Amphion* with his charming Lyre
Begot so sweet a Siren of the air,
That with her Rhetoric made the stones conspire
The ruins of a City to repair,
(A work of wit and reason's wise affair)
    So Love's smooth tongue, the motes such measure taught
    That they joined hands; and so the world was wrought.

### 22

How justly then is Dancing termèd new
Which with the world in point of time begun?
Yea Time itself (whose birth *Jove* never knew
And which is far more ancient than the Sun)
Had not one moment of his age outrun
    When out leapt Dancing from the heap of things,
    And lightly rode upon his nimble wings.

### 23

Reason hath both their pictures in her Treasure,
Where Time the measure of all moving is,
And Dancing is a moving all in measure;
Now if you do resemble that to this
And think both one, I think you think amiss:
    But if you judge them Twins, together got,
    And Time first borne, your judgment erreth not.

## 24

Thus doth it equal age with age enjoy,
And yet in lusty youth for ever flow'rs,
Like Love his Sire, whom Painters make a Boy,
Yet is he eldest of the heav'nly pow'rs;
Or like his brother Time, whose wingèd hours
    Going and coming will not let him die,
    But still preserve him in his infancy."

## 25

This said; the Queen with her sweet lips divine
Gently began to move the subtle air,
Which gladly yielding, did itself incline
To take a shape between those rubies fair
And being formèd, softly did repair
    With twenty doublings in the empty way,
    Unto *Antinous*' ears, and thus did say:

## 26

What eye doth see the heav'n but doth admire
When it the movings of the heav'ns doth see?
Myself, if I to heav'n may once aspire,
If that be dancing, will a Dancer be:
But as for this your frantic jollity
    How it began, or whence you did it learn,
    I never could with reason's eye discern."

## 27

*Antinous* answered: "Jewel of the Earth
Worthy you are that heav'nly Dance to lead:
But for you think our dancing base of birth
And newly borne but of a brain-sick head
I will forthwith his antique Gentry read,
    And for I love him, will his Herald be
    And blaze his arms, and draw his Pedigree.

### 28

When Love had shaped this world, this great fair wight
That all wights else in his wide womb contains,
And had instructed it to dance aright,
A thousand measures with a thousand strains,
Which it should practice with delightful pains
    Until that fatal instant should revolve,
    When all to nothing should again resolve:

### 29

The comely order and proportion fair
On every side did please his wand'ring eye,
Till glancing through the thin transparent air
A rude disordered rout he did espy
Of men and women, that most spitefully
    Did one another throng, and crowd so sore,
    That his kind eye in pity wept therefore.

### 30

And swifter than the Lightning down he came,
Another shapeless Chaos to digest;
He will begin another world to frame,
(For Love till all be well will never rest)
Then with such words as cannot be expressed
    He cuts the troops, that all asunder fling,
    And ere they wist, he casts them in a ring.

### 31

Then did he rarify the Element
And in the center of the ring appear,
The beams that from his forehead shining went,
Begot a horror and religious fear
In all the souls that round about him were,
    Which in their ears attentiveness procures
    While he with such like sounds their minds allures:

### 32

How doth Confusion's Mother, headlong Chance,
Put Reason's noble squadron to the rout?
Or how should you that have the governance
Of Nature's children, heaven and earth throughout
Prescribe them rules, and live yourselves without?
   Why should your fellowship a trouble be,
   Since man's chief pleasure is society?

### 33

If sense hath not yet taught you, learn of me
A comely moderation and discreet,
That your assemblies may well ordered be
When my uniting power shall make you meet;
With heav'nly tunes it shall be tempered sweet:
   And be the model of the world's great frame,
   And you Earth's children, Dancing shall it name.

### 34

Behold the world how it is whirled round,
And for it is so whirled, is namèd so;
In whose large volume many rules are found
Of this new Art, which it doth fairly show:
For your quick eyes in wandering too and fro
   From East to West, on no one thing can glance,
   But if you mark it well, it seems to dance.

### 35

First you see fixed in this huge mirror blue
Of trembling lights a number numberless,
Fixed they are nam'd, but with a name untrue,
For they are moved, and in a Dance express
That great long year that doth contain no less
   Than threescore hundreds of those years in all,
   Which the Sun makes with his course natural.

### 36

What if to you these sparks disordered seem,
As if by chance they had been scattered there?
The Gods a solemn measure do it deem
And see a just proportion everywhere,
And know the points whence first their movings were;
    To which first points when all return again,
    The Axletree of Heav'n[4] shall break in twain.

### 37

Under that spangled sky, five wandering flames,
Besides the King of Day, and Queen of Night,
Are wheeled around, all in their sundry frames,
And all in sundry measures do delight:
Yet altogether keep no measure right.
    For by itself each doth itself advance,
    And by itself each doth a Galliard[5] dance.

### 38

*Venus*, the Mother of that bastard Love,
Which doth usurp the world's great Marshal's name,
Just with the Sun her dainty feet doth move
And unto him doth all her gestures frame:
Now after, now afore, the flattering Dame
    With diverse cunning passages doth err,
    Still him respecting that respects not her.

### 39

For that brave Sun, the Father of the Day,
Doth love this Earth, the Mother of the Night,
And like a reveler in rich array
Doth dance his Galliard in his Lemman's[6] sight,
Both back, and forth, and sideways, passing light;
    His gallant grace doth so the Gods amaze,
    That all stand still and at his beauty gaze.

---

4  The celestial pole round which spins the cosmos
5  A lively dance in triple time
6  Lover or sweetheart

### 40

But see the Earth, when he approcheth near,
How she for joy doth spring and sweetly smile:
But see again her sad and heavy cheer
When changing places he retires a while:
But those black clouds he shortly will exile,
    And make them all before his presence fly
    As mists consumed before his cheerful eye.

### 41

Who doth not see the measures of the Moon
Which thirteen times she danceth every year?
And ends her pavine[7] thirteen times as soon
As doth her brother, of whose golden hair
She borroweth part and proudly doth it wear.
    Then doth she coyly turn her face aside,
    That half her cheek is scarce sometimes descried.

### 42

Next her, the pure, subtle, and cleansing fire,
Is swiftly carried in a circle even:
Though *Vulcan* be pronounced by many a lyre
The only halting God that dwells in heaven.
But that foul name may be more fitly given
    To your false fire that far from heav'n is fall
    And doth consume, waste, spoil, disorder all.

### 43

And now behold your tender Nurse the air
And common neighbor that aye runs around;
How many pictures and impressions fair
Within her empty regions are there found,
Which to your senses Dancing do propound?
    For what are breath, speech, Echos, music, winds,
    But Dancings of the air in sundry kinds?

---

7   A slow processional dance

### 44

For when you breathe, the air in order moves,
Now in, now out, in time and measure true;
And when you speak, so well she dancing loves,
That doubling oft, and oft redoubling new,
With thousand forms she doth herself endue:
    For all the words that from your lips repair,
    Are nought but tricks and turnings of the air.

### 45

Hence is her prattling daughter Echo borne,
That dances to all voices she can hear;
There is no sound so harsh that she doth scorn,
Nor any time wherein she will forbear
The airy pavement with her feet to wear.
    And yet her hearing sense is nothing quick
    For after time she endeth every trick.

### 46

And thou sweet Music, Dancing's only life,
The ear's sole happiness, the air's best speech;
Loadstone of fellowship, charming-rod of strife,
The soft mind's Paradise, the sick mind's Leech,
With thine own tongue thou trees and stones can teach
    That when the Air doth dance her finest measure,
    Then art thou borne the God's and men's sweet pleasure.

### 47

Lastly, where keep the winds their revelry,
Their violent turnings and wild whirling hayes,[8]
But in the Air's translucent gallery?
Where she herself is turned a hundred ways,
While with those Maskers wantonly she plays;
    Yet in this misrule, they such rule embrace
    As two at once encumber not the place.

---

8  A country dance, similar to a reel

### 48

If then fire, air, wand'ring and fixed lights
In every province of th' imperial sky,
Yield perfect forms of dancing to your sights,
In vain I teach the ear, that which the eye
With certain view already doth descry.
   But for your eyes perceive not all they see
   In this I will your senses' master be.

### 49

For lo the Sea that fleets about the Land,
And like a girdle clips her solid waist,
Music and measure both doth understand:
For his great Christall[9] eye is always cast
Up to the Moon, and on her fixèd fast.
   And as she danceth in her pallid sphere,
   So danceth he about his Center here.

### 50

Sometimes his proud green waves in order set,
One after other flow unto the shore,
Which when they have with many kisses wet,
They ebb away in order as before;
And to make known his Courtly Love the more,
   He oft doth lay aside his three-forked Mace,
   And with his arms the timorous Earth embrace.

### 51

Only the Earth doth stand for ever still,
Her rocks remove not, nor her mountains meet,
(Although some wits enriched with Learning's skill
Say heav'n stands firm, and that the Earth doth fleet
And swiftly turneth underneath their feet)
   Yet though the Earth is ever steadfast seen,
   On her broad breast hath Dancing ever been.

---

9  I have retained the older spelling of "crystal" to keep the sacred pun with "Christ" active.

### 52

For those blue veins that through her body spread,
Those sapphire streams which from great hills do spring,
(The Earth's great dugs: for every wight is fed
With sweet fresh moisture from them issuing)
Observe a dance in their wild wandering:
    And still their dance begets a murmur sweet,
    And still the murmur with the dance doth meet.

### 53

Of all their ways I love *Meander's* path,
Which to the tunes of dying Swans doth dance,
Such winding sleights, such turns and tricks he hath,
Such Creeks, such wrenches, and such dalliance,
That whether it be hap or heedless chance,
    In his indented course and wriggling play
    He seems to dance a perfect cunning Hay.[10]

### 54

But wherefore do these streams for ever run?
To keep themselves for ever sweet and clear:
For let their everlasting course be done
They straight corrupt and foul with mud appear.
O ye sweet Nymphs that beauty's loss do fear,
    Contemn the Drugs that Physic doth devise,
    And learn of Love this dainty exercise.

### 55

See how those flowers that have sweet Beauty too
(The only Jewels that the Earth doth wear
When the young Sun in bravery her doth woo)
As oft as they the whistling wind doth hear,
Do wave their tender bodies here and there;
    And though their dance no perfect measure is,
    Yet oftentimes their music makes them kiss.

---

10  See *hayes* in Stanza 47.

### 56

What makes the Vine about the Elm to dance
With turnings, windings, and embracements round?
What makes the Load-stone to the North advance
His subtle point, as if from thence he found
His chief attractive Virtue to redound?
    Kind Nature first doth cause all things to love,
    Love makes them dance and in just order move.


### 57

Hark how the Birds do sing, and mark then how
Jump with the modulation of their lays,
They lightly leap, and skip from bow to bow;
Yet do the Cranes deserve a greater praise
Which keep such measure in their airy ways,
    As when they all in order rankèd are,
    They make a perfect form triangular.


### 58

In the chief angle flies the watchful guide,
And all the followers their heads do lay
On their foregoers' backs, on either side,
But for the Captain hath no rest to stay
His head forwearied with the windy way,
    He back retires, and then the next behind,
    As his Lieutenant leads them through the wind.


### 59

But why relate I every singular?
Since all the World's great fortunes and affairs
Forward and backward rapt and whirled are,
According to the music of the spheres:
And Chance herself, her nimble feet upbears
    On a round slippery wheel that rolleth aye,
    And turns all states with her impetuous sway.

### 60

Learn then to dance, you that are Princes borne
And lawful Lords of earthly creatures all,
Imitate them, and thereof take no scorn,
For this new Art to them is natural—
And imitate the stars celestial:
    For when pale Death your vital twist shall sever,
    Your better parts must dance with them for ever.

### 61

Thus Love persuades, and all the crowd of men
That stands around doth make a murmuring;
As when the wind loosed from his hollow den,
Among the trees a gentle bass doth sing,
Or as a Brook through pebbles wandering:
    But in their looks they uttered this plain speech,
    That they would learn to dance if Love would teach.

### 62

Then first of all, he doth demonstrate plain
The motions seven that are in Nature found,
Upward and downward, forth and back again,
To this side and to that, and turning round:
Whereof, a thousand brawls he doth compound,
    Which he doth teach unto the multitude,
    And ever with a turn they must conclude.

### 63

As when a Nymph arising from the Land
Leadeth a dance with her long watery train
Down to the Sea, she wries[11] to every hand
And every way doth cross the fertile plain:
But when at last she falls into the main
    Then all her troubles concluded are,
    And with the Sea her course is circular.

---

11  To twist or writhe

### 64

Thus when at first Love had them marshalèd
As erst he did the shapeless mass of things,
He taught them rounds and winding Hayes to tread,
And about trees to cast themselves in rings.
As the two Bears whom the first mover flings
    With a short turn about heaven's Axletree,
    In a round dance for ever wheeling be.

### 65

But after these, as men more civil grew
He did more grave and solemn measures frame,
With such fair order and proportion true
And correspondence every way the same
That no fault-finding eye did ever blame:
    For every eye was movèd at the sight
    With sober wond'ring, and with sweet delight.

### 66

Not those old Students of the heavenly book,
*Atlas* the great, *Prometheus* the wise,
Which on the Stars did all their life-time look
Could ever find such measures in the skies,
So full of change and rare varieties;
    Yet all the feet whereon these measures go,
    Are only Spondees, solemn, grave, and slow.

### 67

But for more diverse and more pleasing show,
A swift and wand'ring dance she did invent,
With passages uncertain to and fro,
Yet with a certain answer and consent
To the quick music of the Instrument.
    Five was the number of the Music's feet,
    Which still the dance did with five paces meet.

## 68

A gallant dance, that lively doth bewray[12]
A spirit and a virtue Masculine,
Impatient that her house on earth should stay
Since she herself is fiery and divine:
Oft doth she make her body upward fline,[13]
    With lofty turns and caprioles[14] in the air,
    Which with the lusty tunes accordeth fair.

## 69

What shall I name those courante[15] travases[16]
That on a triple Dactyl foot do run
Close by the ground with sliding passages,
Wherein that Dancer greatest praise hath won
Which with best order can all orders shun:
    For everywhere he wantonly must range,
    And turn and wind, with unexpected change.

## 70

Yet is there one, the most delightful kind,
A lofty jumping, or a leaping round,
Where arm in arm, two Dancers are entwined,
And whirl themselves with strict embracements bound,
And still their feet an Anapest do sound:
    An Anapest is all their music's song,
    Whose first two feet are short, and third is long.

---

12  Divulge or betray
13  Fly
14  A particular dance move
15  A swift, gliding dance
16  Traversers, another movement in dance

## 71

As the victorious twins of *Leda* and *Jove*
That taught the Spartans dancing on the sands
Of swift *Eurotas*[17] dance in Heav'n above,
Knit and united with eternal hands;
Among the Stars their double Image stands,
    Where both are carried with an equal pace
    Together jumping in their turning race.

## 72

This is the Net wherein the Sun's bright eye
*Venus* and *Mars* entangled did behold;
For in this Dance, their arms they so imply
As each doth seem the other to enfold:
What if lewd wits another tale have told
    Of jealous *Vulcan*, and of iron chains,
    Yet this true sense that forgèd lie contains.

## 73

These various forms of dancing Love did frame,
And beside these, a hundred millions moe,[18]
And as he did invent, he taught the same
With goodly gesture, and with comely show,
Now keeping state, now humbly honoring low:
    And ever for the persons and the place
    He taught most fit, and best according grace.

## 74

For Love within his fertile working brain
Did then conceive those gracious Virgins three
Whose civil moderation does maintain
All decent order and conveniency,
And fair respect, and seemly modesty:
    And then he thought it fit they should be born,
    That their sweet presence dancing might adorn.

---

17    A river in Thessaly, Greece. There may be more mythological significance that is unknown.
18    More

75

Hence is it that these Graces painted are
With hand in hand, dancing an endless round:
And with regarding eyes, that still beware
That there be no disgrace amongst them found;
With equal foot they beat the flow'ry ground,
　Laughing, or singing, as their passions will,
　Yet nothing that they do becomes them ill.

76

Thus Love taught men, and men thus learned of Love
Sweet Music's sound with feet to counterfeit,
Which was long time before high thundering *Jove*
Was lifted up to heav'n's imperial seat.
For though by birth he were the Prince of *Crete*,
　Nor *Crete*, nor Heav'n should the young Prince have seen
　If Dancers with their Timbrels had not been.

77

Since when all ceremonious mysteries,
All sacred Orgies and religious rites,
All pomps, and triumphs, and solemnities,
All Funerals, Nuptials, and like public sights,
All Parliaments of peace, and warlike fights,
　Al learnèd Arts, and every great affair
　A lively shape of Dancing seems to bear.

78

For what did he who with his ten-tongued Lute
Gave Beasts and blocks an understanding ear?
Or rather into bestial minds and brute
Shed and infused the beams of reason clear?
Doubtless for men that rude and savage were
　A civil form of dancing he devised,
　Wherewith unto their Gods they sacrificed.

### 79

So did *Musaeus*, so *Amphion* did,
And *Linus* with his sweet enchanting song,
And he whose hand the earth of monsters rid
And had men's ears fast chainèd to his tongue:
And *Theseus* to his wood-born slaves among
    Used dancing as the finest policy
    To plant religion and society.

### 80

And therefore now the Thracian *Orpheus* Lyre
And *Hercules* himself are stellified;
And in high heav'n amidst the starry Choir
Dancing their parts continually do slide:
So on the Zodiac *Ganymede* doth ride,
    And so is *Hebe* with the Muses nine
    For pleasing *Jove* with dancing, made divine.

### 81

Wherefore was *Proteus* said himself to change
Into a stream, a Lion, and a tree,
And many other forms fantastic, strange,
As in his fickle thought he wished to be?
But that he danced with such facility.
    As like a Lion he could pace with pride,
    Ply like a Plant, and like a River slide.

### 82

And how was *Caeneus* made at first a man,
And then a woman, then a man again
But in a Dance? which when he first began
He the man's part in measure did sustain
But when he changed into a second strain
    He danced the woman's part another space
    And then returned into his former place.

### 83

Hence sprang the fable of *Tiresias*
That he the pleasure of both sexes tried;
For in a dance he man and woman was
By often change of place from side to side:
But for the woman easily did slide
    And smoothly swim with cunning hidden Art,
    He took more pleasure in a woman's part.

### 84

So to a fish *Venus* herself did change,
And swimming through the soft and yielding wave,
With gentle motions did so smoothly range
As none might see where she the water drave:
But this plain truth that falsèd fable gave
    That she did dance with sliding easiness,
    Pliant and quick in wand'ring passages,

### 85

And merry *Bacchus* practiced dancing too,
And to the Lydian numbers rounds did make:
The like he did in th' Eastern India do,
And taught them all when *Phœbus* did awake,
And when at night he did his Coach forsake:
    To honor heav'n, and heav'n's great rolling eye
    With turning dances, and with melody.

### 86

Thus they who first did found a common-weal,
And they who first Religion did ordain,
By dancing first the people's hearts did steal,
Of whom we now a thousand tales do feign.
Yet do we now their perfect rules retain,
    And use them still in such devises new
    As in the World, long since their with'ring, grew.

87

For after Towns and Kingdoms founded were
Between great States arose well-ordered War;
Wherein most perfect measure doth appear
Whether their well-set ranks respected are
In Quadrant form or Semicircular:
    Or else the March, when all the troops advance
    And to the Drum, in gallant order dance.

88

And after Wars, when white-winged Victory
Is with a glorious triumph beautified,
And every one doth *Io, Io* cry,
Whiles all in gold the Conqueror doth ride,
The solemn pomp that fills the City wide
    Observes such rank and measure everywhere,
    As if they altogether dancing were.

89

The like just order Mourners do observe,
(But with unlike affection and attire)
When some great man that nobly did deserve
And whom his friends impatiently desire
Is brought with honor to his latest fire:
    The dead corpse too in that sad dance is moved,
    As if both dead and living, dancing loved.

90

A diverse cause, but like solemnity
Unto the Temple leads the bashful bride,
Which blusheth like the Indian Ivory
Which is with dip of Tyrian purple died:
A golden troop doth pass on every side
    Of flourishing young men and Virgins gay,
    Which keep fair measure all the flow'ry way.

### 91

And not alone the general multitude,
But those choice *Nestors* which in counsel grave
Of Cities, and of Kingdoms do conclude,
Most comely order in their Sessions have:
Wherefore the wise Thessalians ever gave
    The name of Leader of their Country's dance
    To him that had their Country's governance.

### 92

And those great Masters of the liberal Arts
In all their several Schools do Dancing teach:
For humble Grammar first doth set the parts
Of congruent and well-according speech:
Which Rhetoric, whose state the clouds doth reach,
    And heav'nly Poetry do forward lead,
    And diverse Measures diversely do tread.

### 93

For Rhetoric, clothing speech in rich array
In looser numbers teacheth her to range,
With twenty tropes, and turning every way,
And various figures, and licentious change:
But Poetry with rule and order strange
    So curiously doth move each single pace,
    As all is marred if she one foot misplace.

### 94

These Arts of speech the guides and Marshals are,
But Logic leadeth Reason in a Dance,
(Reason the Cynosure[19] and bright Load-star
In this world's Sea t'avoid the rock of Chance)
For with close following and continuance
    One reason doth another so ensue,
    As in conclusion still the dance is true.

---

19   The Pole Star, in the constellation Ursa Minor

### 95

So Music to her own sweet tunes doth trip
With tricks of 3, 5, 8, 15, and more:
So doth the Art of Numb'ring seem to skip
From ev'n to odd in her proportioned score:
So do those skills, whose quick eyes do explore
    The just dimension both of Earth and Heav'n,
    In all their rules observe a measure ev'n.

### 96

Lo this is Dancing's true nobility,
Dancing, the child of Music and of Love;
Dancing itself, both love and harmony,
Where all agree, and all in order move;
Dancing the Art that all Arts do approve:
    The fair Character of the world's consent,
    The heav'n's true figure, and th' earth's ornament."

### 97

The Queen, whose dainty ears had borne too long
The tedious praise of that she did despise,
Adding once more the music of the tongue
To the sweet speech of her alluring eyes,
Began to answer in such winning wise
    As that forthwith *Antinous'* tongue was tied,
    His eyes fast fixed, his ears were open wide.

### 98

Forsooth" (quoth she) "great glory you have won
To your trim Minion Dancing all this while,
By blazing him Love's first begotten son;
Of every ill the hateful Father vile
That doth the world with sorceries beguile:
    Cunningly mad, religiously profane,
    Wit's monster, Reason's canker, Sense's bane.

### 99

Love taught the mother that unkind desire
To wash her hands in her own Infant's blood;
Love taught the daughter to betray her Sire
Into most base unworthy servitude;
Love taught the brother to prepare such food
    To feast his brothers that the all-seeing Sun,
      Wrapped in a cloud, that wicked sight did shun.

### 100

And even this self same Love hath dancing taught,
An Art that showeth th' *Idea* of his mind
With vainness, frenzy, and misorder fraught;
Sometimes with blood and cruelties unkind:
For in a dance, *Tereus'* mad wife did find
    Fit time and place by murdering her son,
      T'avenge the wrong his traitorous Sire had done.

### 101

What mean the Mermaids when they dance and sing
But certain death unto the Mariner?
What tidings do the dancing Dolphins bring
But that some dangerous storm approacheth near?
Then since both Love and Dancing liveries bear
    Of such ill hap, unhappy may they prove,
      That sitting free, will either dance or love."

### 102

Yet once again *Antinous* did reply,
"Great Queen, condemn not Love the innocent,
For this mischievous lust, which traitorously
Usurps his Name, and steals his ornament:
For that true Love which dancing did invent,
    Is he that tuned the world's whole harmony,
      And linked all men in sweet society.

### 103

He first extracted from th' earth-mingled mind
That heav'nly fire, or quintessence divine,
Which doth such sympathy in beauty find
As is between the Elm and fruitful Vine,
And so to beauty ever doth incline.
   Life's life it is, and cordial to the heart,
    And of our better part, the better part.

### 104

This is true Love, by that true *Cupid* got
Which danceth Galliards in your amorous eyes,
But to your frozen heart approacheth not,
Only your heart he dares not enterprise.
And yet through every other part he flies,
   And everywhere he nimbly danceth now.
    That in yourself, yourself perceive not how.

### 105

For your sweet beauty daintily transfused
With due proportion throughout every part,
What is it but a dance where Love hath used
His finer cunning, and more curious Art?
Where all the Elements themselves impart,
   And turn, and wind, and mingle with such measure,
    That th' eye that sees it, surfeits with the pleasure?

### 106

Love in the twinkling of your eyelids danceth,
Love danceth in your pulses and your veins,
Love when you sew, your needle's point advanceth,
And makes it dance a thousand curious strains
Of winding rounds, whereof the form remains,
   To show, that your fair hands can dance the Hay,
    Which your fine feet would learn as well as they.

### 107

And when your Ivory fingers touch the strings
Of any silver-sounding instrument,
Love makes them dance to those sweet murmurings,
With busy skill, and cunning excellent:
O that your feet those tunes would represent
    With artificial motions to and fro,
      That Love this Art in every part might show.

### 108

Yet your fair soul which came from heav'n above,
To rule this house, another heav'n below,
With diverse pow'rs in harmony doth move,
And all the virtues that from her do flow,
In a round measure hand in hand do go.
    Could I now see as I conceive this Dance,
      Wonder and Love would cast me in a trance.

### 109

The richest Jewel in all the heav'nly Treasure
That ever yet unto the Earth was shown,
Is perfect Concord, th' only perfect pleasure
That wretched Earth-borne men have ever known,
For many hearts it doth compound in one:
    That when so one doth will, or speak, or do,
      With one consent they all agree thereto.

### 110

Concord's true picture shineth in this Art,
Where diverse men and women rankèd be,
And every one doth dance a sev'ral part,
Yet all as one, in measure do agree,
Observing perfect uniformity:
    All turn together, all together trace,
      And all together honor and embrace.

### 111

If they whom sacred Love hath linked in one,
Do, as they dance, in all their course of life
Never shall burning grief nor bitter moan,
Nor factious difference, nor unkind strife,
Arise betwixt the husband and the wife.
   For whether forth or back, or round he go,
   As the man doth, so must the woman do.

### 112

What if by often interchange of place
Sometime the woman gets the upper hand?
That is but done for more delightful grace,
For on that part she doth not ever stand:
But as the Measure's law doth her command
   She wheels about, and ere the dance doth end,
   Into her former place she doth transcend.

### 113

But not alone this correspondence meet
And uniform consent doth dancing praise,
For Comeliness the child of order sweet
Enamels it with her eye-pleasing rays:
Fair Comeliness, ten hundred thousand ways
   Through dancing sheds itself, and makes it shine
   With glorious beauty, and with grace divine.

### 114

For Comeliness is a disposing fair
Of things and actions in fit time and place,
Which doth in dancing show itself most clear,
When troops confused which here and there do trace
Without distinguishment or bounded space,
   By dancing's rule, into such ranks are brought,
   As glads the eye, as ravisheth the thought.

### 115

Then why should reason judge that reasonless
Which is wit's offspring, and the work of Art,
Image of concord, and of comeliness.
Who sees a clock moving in every part,
A sailing Pinnace,[20] or a wheeling Cart,
　　But thinks that reason ere it came to pass
　　The first impulsive cause and mover was?

### 116

Who sees an Army all in rank advance
But deems a wise Commander is in place
Which leadeth on that brave victorious dance?
Much more in dancing's Art, in dancing's grace
Blindness itself may reason's footstep trace:
　　For of Love's Maze it is the curious plot,
　　And of man's fellowship the true-love knot.

### 117

But if these eyes of yours, (Load-stars of love
Showing the world's great dance to your mind's eye)
Cannot with all their demonstrations move
Kind apprehension in your fantasy
Of Dancing's virtue, and nobility:
　　How can my barbarous tongue win you thereto
　　Which heav'n and earth's fair speech could never do?

### 118

O Love my King: If all my wit and power
Have done you all the service that they can,
O be you present in this present hour,
And help your servant and your true Liege-man
End that persuasion which I erst began:
　　For who in praise of dancing can persuade
　　With such sweet force as Love, which dancing made."

---

20　A small boat

### 119

Love heard his prayer, and swifter than the wind
Like to a page, in habit, face, and speech,
He came, and stood *Antinous* behind,
And many secrets to his thoughts did teach.
At last, a christall Mirror he did reach
   Unto his hands, that he with one rash view,
   All forms therein by Love's revealing knew.

### 120

And humbly honoring, gave it to the Queen
With this faire speech: "See fairest Queen" (quoth he)
"The fairest sight that ever shall be seen,
And th' only wonder of posterity,
The richest work in Nature's treasury;
   Which she disdains to show on this world's stage,
   And thinks it far too good for our rude age.

### 121

But in another world divided far,
In the great, fortunate, triangled Isle,
Thrice twelve degrees removed from the North star
She will this glorious workmanship compile
Which she hath been conceiving all this while
   Since the world's birth, and will bring forth at last,
   When six and twenty hundred years are past."

### 122

*Penelope* the Queen when she had viewed
The strange-eye-dazzling-admirable sight,
Fain would have praised the state and pulchritude,
But she was stricken dumb with wonder quite,
Yet her sweet mind retained her thinking might:
   Her ravished mind in heav'nly thoughts did dwell,
   But what she thought, no mortal tongue can tell.

### 123

You Lady Muse, whom *Jove* the Counselor
Begot of Memory, wisdom's Treasuress,
To your divining tongue is given a power
Of uttering secrets large and limitless:
You can *Penelope's* strange thoughts express
    Which she conceived, and then would fain have told,
    When she the wondrous Christall did behold.

### 124

Her wingèd thoughts bore up her mind so high
As that she weened she saw the glorious throne
Where the bright moon doth sit in majesty,
A thousand sparkling stars about her shone,
But she herself did sparkle more alone
    Then all those thousand beauties would have done
    If they had been confounded all in one.

### 125

And yet she thought those stars moved in such measure
To do their Sovereign honor and delight,
As soothed her mind with sweet enchanting pleasure
Although the various change amazed her sight,
And her weak judgement did entangle quite:
    Beside, their moving made them shine more clear,
    As Diamonds moved more sparkling do appear.

### 126

This was the Picture of her wondrous thought;
But who can wonder that her thought was so,
Since *Vulcan* King of fire, that Mirror wrought
(Who things to come, present, and past doth know)
And there did represent in lively show;
    Our glorious English Courts divine Image
    As it should be in this our golden age.

### 127

Away, *Terpsichore*, light Muse away,
And come *Urania*,[21] Prophetess divine;
Come Muse of heav'n, my burning thirst allay,
Even now, for want of sacred drink I tine.[22]
In heav'nly moisture dip this Pen of mine,
    And let my mouth with Nectar overflow,
    For I must more than mortal glory show.

### 128

O that I had *Homer's* abundant vein,
I would hereof another *Ilias* make,
Or else the man of *Mantua's*[23] charmèd brain
In whose large throat great *Jove* the thunder spake.
O that I could old *Geoffrey's*[24] Muse awake,
    Or borrow *Colin's*[25] fair heroic stile,
    Or smooth my rhymes with *Delia's* servant's[26] file.

### 129

O could I, sweet Companion, sing like you,
Which, of a shadow, under a shadow sing;
Or like *Salices'* sad lover true,
Or like the Bee, the Marigold's darling,
Whose sudden verse Love covers with his wing:[27]
    O that your brains were mingled all with mine,
    T'enlarge my wit for this great work divine.

---

21   Muse of astronomy/astrology
22   To suffer deprivation
23   Vergil
24   Geoffrey Chaucer
25   Colin Clout was a sobriquet for Edmund Spenser
26   English poet, and Davies' contemporary, Samuel Daniel
27   The three poets from Davies' own circle referenced in these lines are not identifiable
with any certainty

### 130

Yet *Astrophel*[28] might one for all suffice,
Whose supple Muse Chameleon-like doth change
Into all forms of excellent device:
So might the Swallow,[29] whose swift Muse doth range
Through rare *Ideas*, and inventions strange,
 And ever doth enjoy her joyful spring,
 And sweeter than the Nightingale doth sing.

### 131

O that I might that singing Swallow hear
To whom I owe my service and my love,
His sugared tunes would so enchant mine ear,
And in my mind such sacred fury move,
As I should knock at heav'n's great gate above
 With my proud rhymes, while of this heav'nly state
 I do aspire the shadows to relate.

## FINIS.

*So ends the first edition from 1596. The following alternative (and unfinished)*
*conclusion is found in the second edition from 1622.*

---

28 Sir Philip Sidney
29 Richard Martin, to whom the poem is dedicated

[127.]

Her[30] brighter dazzling beams of majesty
Were laid aside, for she vouchsafed awhile
With gracious, cheerful, and familiar eye
Upon the revels of her Court to smile;
For so Time's Journeys she doth oft beguile:
    Like sight no mortal eye might elsewhere see,
    So full of State, Art, and variety.


[128.]

For of her barons brave, and ladies fair—
Who had they been elsewhere, most fair had been;
Many an incomparable lovely pair,
With hand in hand were interlinkèd seen,
Making faire honour to their sovereign Queen;
    Forward they paced, and did their pace apply
    To a most sweet and solemn melody.


[129.]

So subtle and curious was the measure,
With such unlooked for change in every strain;
As that *Penelope* rapt with sweet pleasure,
Weened she beheld the true proportion plain
Of her own web, weaved and unweaved again;
    But that her art was somewhat less she thought,
    And on a mere ignoble subject wrought.


[130.]

For here like to the silkworm's industry,
Beauty itself out of itself did weave
So rare a work, and of such subtlety,
As did all eyes entangle and deceive,
And in all minds a strange impression leave;
    In this sweet labyrinth did *Cupid* stray,
    And never had the power to pass away.

---

30   Queen Elizabeth

[131.]

As when the Indians, neighbors of the morning,
In honour of the cheerful rising sun;
With pearl and painted plumes themselves adorning,
A solemn stately measure have begun;
The god well pleased with that fair honor done,
   Sheds forth his beams, and doth their faces kiss
   With that immortal glorious face of his.

[132.]

So, &c., &c.

# Nosce Teipsum
(1599)

## Royal Dedication

*TO MY MOST GRACIOUS DREAD SOVEREIGN.*

To that clear majesty which in the North
*Doth, like another Sun in glory rise*;
Which standeth fix'd, yet spreads her *heav'nly worth*;
Lodestone to hearts, and lodestar to all eyes.

Like Heav'n in all; like th' Earth in this alone,
That though great States by her support do stand,
Yet she herself supported is of none,
But by th' finger of th' Almighty's hand:

To th' divinest and th' richest mind,
Both by Art's purchase and by Nature's dower,
That ever was from Heav'n to Earth confin'd,
To show th' utmost of a creature's power:

To that great Spirit, which doth great kingdoms move,
Th' sacred spring whence *right* and *honor* streams,
Distilling *Virtue*, shedding *Peace* and *Love*,
In ev'ry place, as *Cynthia* sheds her beams:

I offer up some sparkles of that fire,
Whereby we *reason, live, and move, and be*;
These sparks by nature evermore aspire,
Which makes them to so *high* a *highness* flee.

Fair *Soul*, since to th' fairest body knit,
You give such lively life, such quick'ning power,
Such sweet celestial influences to it,
As keeps it still in youth's immortal flower:

(As where th' sun is present all th' year,
And never doth retire his golden ray,
Needs must th' Spring be everlasting there,
And ev'ry season like th' month of May.)

O! many, many years may you remain,
A happy angel to this happy Land;
Long, long may you on Earth our empress reign,
Ere you in Heav'n a glorious angel stand.

Stay long (sweet spirit) ere thou to Heav'n depart,
Which makes each place a heav'n wherein thou art.

Her Majesty's least and
unworthiest Subject,
JOHN DAVIES.


**Another dedication of a gift-copy (in ms.) in the possession of his grace the Duke of Northumberland at Alnwick Castle**

*TO THE RIGHT NOBLE, VALOROUS, AND LEARNED
PRINCE HENRY, EARL OF NORTHUMBERLAND:*

The strongest and the noblest argument
   To prove the soul immortal, rests in this:
   That in no mortal thing it finds content,
   But seeks an object that eternal is.
If any soul hath this immortal sign,
   (As every soul doth show it, more or less),
   It is your spirit, heroic and divine;
   Which this true note most lively doth express;
For being a prince, and having princely blood,
   The noblest of all Europe in your veins;
   Having youth, wealth, pleasure, and every good,
   Which all the world doth seek, with endless pains.
Yet can you never fix your thoughts on these,
   These cannot with your heav'nly mind agree;
   These momentary objects cannot please,
   Your wingèd spirit, which more aloft doth flee.
It only longs to learn and know the truth,
   The truth of every thing, which never dies;
   The nectar which preserves the soul in youth;
   The manna which doth minds immortalize.

These noble studies, more ennoble you,
   And bring more honor to your race and name
   Than Hotspur's fire, which did the Scots subdue,
   Than Brabant's scion, or great Charles his name.
Then to what spirit shall I these notes commend,
   But unto that which doth them best express;
   Who will to them more kind protection lend,
   Than He which did protect me in distress?

# Nosce Teipsum

## *Of Human Knowledge.*

hy did my parents send me to the Schools,
That I with knowledge might enrich my mind?
Since the *desire to know* first made men fools,
And did corrupt the root of all mankind:                4

For when God's hand had written in the hearts
Of the first Parents, all the rules of good,
So that their skill infused did pass all arts
That ever were, before, or since the Flood;             8

And when their reason's eye was sharp and clear,
And (as an eagle can behold the sun)
Could have approached th' Eternal Light as near,
As the intellectual angels could have done:            12

Even then to them the *Spirit of Lies* suggests
That they were blind, because they saw not ill;
And breathes into their uncorrupted breasts
A curious *wish*, which did corrupt their *will*.       16

For that same ill they straight desired to know;
Which ill, being nought but a defect of good,
In all God's works the devil could not show
While Man their lord in his perfection stood.          20

So that themselves were first to do the ill,
Ere they thereof the knowledge could attain;
Like him that knew not poison's power to kill,
Until (by tasting it) himself was slain.               24

Even so by tasting of that fruit forbid,
Where they sought *knowledge*, they did *error* find;
Ill they desired to know, and ill they did;
And to give *Passion* eyes, made *Reason* blind.       28

For then their minds did first in Passion see
Those wretched shapes of *Misery* and *Woe*,
Of *Nakedness*, of *Shame*, of *Poverty*,
Which then their own experience made them know.　　32

But then grew *Reason* dark, that *she* no more,
Could the fair forms of *Good* and *Truth* discern;
*Bats* they became, that *eagles* were before:
And this they got by their *desire to learn*.　　36

But we their wretched offspring, what do we?
Do not we still taste of the fruit forbid
While with fond fruitless curiosity,
In books profane we seek for knowledge hid?　　40

What is this *knowledge* but the sky-stolen fire,
For which the *thief* still chained in ice doth sit?
And which the poor rude *Satyr* did admire,
And needs would kiss but burnt his lips with it.　　44

What is it? but the cloud of empty rain,
Which when *Jove's* guest embraced, he monsters got?
Or the false *pails* which oft being filled with pain,
Received the water, but retained it not!　　48

Shortly, what is it but the fiery coach
Which the *Youth* sought, and sought his death withal?
Or the *boy's* wings, which when he did approach
The *sun's* hot beams, did melt and let him fall?　　52

And yet alas, when all our lamps are burned,
Our bodies wasted, and our spirits spent;
When we have all the learnèd volumes turned,
Which yield men's wits both help and ornament:　　56

What can we know? or what can we discern?
When *Error* chokes the windows of the mind,
The diverse forms of things, how can we learn,
That have been ever from our birthday blind?　　60

When *Reason's* lamp, which (like the *sun* in sky)
Throughout *Man's* little world her beams did spread;
Is now become a sparkle, which doth lie
Under the ashes, half extinct, and dead:                    64

How can we hope, that through the eye and ear,
This dying sparkle, in this cloudy place,
Can recollect these beams of knowledge clear,
Which were infused in the first minds by grace?             68

So might the heir whose father hath in play
Wasted a thousand pound of ancient rent;
By painful earning of a groat a day,
Hope to restore the patrimony spent.                        72

The wits that dived most deep and soared most high
Seeking Man's powers, have found his weakness such:
"Skill comes so slow, and life so fast doth fly,
"We learn so little and forget so much.                     76

For this the wisest of all moral men
Said, '*He knew nought, but that he nought did know*';
And the great mocking-Master mocked not then,
When he said, '*Truth was buried deep below.*'              80

For how may we to others' things attain,
When none of us his own soul understands?
For which the Devil mocks our curious brain,
When, '*Know thyself*' his oracle commands.                 84

For why should we the busy Soul believe,
When boldly she concludes of that and this;
When of herself she can no judgment give,
Nor how, nor whence, nor where, nor what she is?            88

All things without, which round about we see,
We seek to know, and how therewith to do;
But that whereby we *reason, live, and be,*
Within ourselves, we strangers are thereto.                 92

We seek to know the moving of each sphere,
And the strange cause of th' ebbs and floods of *Nile*;
But of that clock within our breasts we bear,
The subtle motions we forget the while.                    96

We that acquaint ourselves with every *Zone*
And pass both *Tropics* and behold the *Poles*,
When we come home, are to ourselves unknown,
And unacquainted still with our own *Souls*.               100

We study *Speech* but others we persuade;
We *leech-craft* learn, but others cure with it;
We interpret *laws*, which other men have made,
But read not those which in our hearts are writ.           104

Is it because the mind is like the eye,
Through which it gathers knowledge by degrees—
Whose rays reflect not, but spread outwardly:
Not seeing itself when other things it sees?               108

No, doubtless; for the mind can backward cast
Upon herself, her understanding light;
But she is so corrupt, and so defaced,
As her own image doth herself affright.                    112

As in the fable of the Lady fair,
Which for her lust was turned into a cow;
When thirsty to a stream she did repair,
And saw herself transformed she wist not how:              116

At first she startles, then she stands amazed,
At last with terror she from thence doth fly;
And loathes the watery glass wherein she gazed,
And shuns it still, though she for thirst do die:          120

Even so *Man's Soul* which did God's image bear,
And was at first fair, good, and spotless pure;
Since with her sins her beauties blotted were,
Doth of all sights her own sight least endure:             124

For even at first reflection she espies,
Such strange *chimeras*, and such monsters there;
Such toys, such *antics*, and such vanities,
As she retires, and shrinks for shame and fear.        128

And as the man loves least at home to be,
That hath a sluttish house haunted with *spirits*;
So she, impatient her own faults to see,
Turns from herself and in strange things delights.        132

For this few *know themselves*: for merchants broke
View their estate with discontent and pain;
And seas are troubled, when they do revoke
Their flowing waves into themselves again.        136

And while the face of outward things we find,
Pleasing and fair, agreeable and sweet;
These things transport, and carry out the mind,
That with herself herself can never meet.        140

Yet if *Affliction* once her wars begin,
And threat the feebler *Sense* with sword and fire;
The *Mind* contracts herself and shrinketh in,
And to herself she gladly doth retire.        144

As *Spiders* touched, seek their web's inmost part;
As *bees* in storms unto their hives return;
As blood in danger gathers to the heart;
As men seek towns, when foes the country burn.        148

If aught can teach us aught, *Affliction's* looks,
(Making us look into ourselves so near,)
Teach us to *know ourselves* beyond all books,
Or all the learned Schools that ever were.        152

This *mistress* lately plucked me by the ear,
And many a golden lesson hath me taught;
Hath made my *Senses* quick, and Reason clear,
Reformed my Will and rectified my Thought.        156

So do the *winds* and *thunders* cleanse the air;
So working lees settle and purge the wine;
So lopped and prunèd trees do flourish fair;
So doth the fire the drossy gold refine. 160

Neither *Minerva* nor the learnèd Muse,
Nor rules of *Art*, nor *precepts* of the wise,
Could in my brain those beams of skill infuse,
As but the glance of this *Dame's* angry eyes. 164

She within *lists* my ranging mind hath brought,
That now beyond myself I list not go;
Myself am *center* of my circling thought,
Only *myself* I study, learn, and know. 168

I know my body's of so frail a kind,
As force without, fevers within can kill;
I know the heavenly nature of my mind,
But 'tis corrupted both in wit and will: 172

I know my *Soul* hath power to know all things,
Yet is she blind and ignorant in all;
I know I am one of Nature's little kings,
Yet to the least and vilest things am thrall. 176

I know my life's a pain and but a span,
I know my *Sense* is mocked with every thing:
And to conclude, I know myself a MAN,
Which is a *proud*, and yet a *wretched* thing. 180

### Of the Soul of Man and the Immortality thereof.

The *lights of heav'n* (which are the World's fair eyes)
Look down into the World, the World to see;
And as they turn, or wander in the skies,
Survey all things that on this *Center* be. 184

And yet the *lights* which in my *tower* do shine,
Mine eyes which view all objects, nigh and far;
Look not into this little world of mine,
Nor see my face, wherein they fixèd are. 188

Since *Nature* fails us in no needful thing,
Why want I means my inward self to see?
Which sight the knowledge of myself might bring,
Which to true wisdom is the first degree.                    192

That *Power* which gave me eyes the World to view,
To see myself infused an *inward* light;
Whereby my *Soul*, as by a mirror true,
Of her own form may take a perfect sight.                    196

But as the sharpest *eye* discerneth nought,
Except the *sun*-beams in the air do shine;
So the best *Soul* with her reflecting thought,
Sees not herself without some light divine.                  200

*O Light* which mak'st the light, which makes the day!
Which set'st the eye without, and mind within;
Lighten my spirit with one clear heavenly ray,
Which now to view itself doth first begin.                   204

For her true form how can my spark discern?
Which dim by *nature*, *Art* did never clear;
When the great wits, of whom all skill we learn,
Are ignorant both *what* she is, and *where*.                208

One thinks the *Soul* is *air*; another, *fire*;
Another *blood*, diffused about the heart;
Another saith, the *elements* conspire,
And to her *essence* each doth give a part.                  212

*Musicians* think our *Souls* are *harmonies*,
*Physicians* hold that they *complexions* be;
*Epicures* make them swarms of *atomies*,
Which do by chance into our bodies flee.                     216

Some think one general *Soul* fills every brain,
As the bright *sun* sheds light in every star;
And others think the name of *Soul* is vain,
And that we only *well-mixed* bodies are.                    220

In judgment of her *substance* thus they vary;
And thus they vary in judgment of her *seat*;
For some her chair up to the brain do carry,
Some thrust it down into the *stomach's* heat.                    224

Some place it in the root of life, the *heart*;
Some in the *liver*, fountain of the veins;
Some say, *She is all in all, and all in part*:
Some say, She is not contained but all contains.                    228

Thus these great clerks their little wisdom show,
While with their doctrines they at *hazard* play,
Tossing their light opinions to and fro,
To mock the *lewd*, as learn'd in this as they.                    232

For no crazed brain could ever yet propound,
Touching the *Soul*, so vain and fond a thought,
But some among these masters have been found,
Which in their *Schools* the self-same thing have taught.                    236

*God only wise*, to punish pride of wit,
Among men's wits hath this confusion wrought,
As the proud *tower* whose points the clouds did hit,
By tongues' confusion was to ruin brought.                    240

But *Thou* which didst *Man's soul* of nothing make,
And when to nothing it was fallen again,
"To make it new, the form of man didst take,
"And *God* with *God*, becam'st a *Man* with men.                    244

Thou, that hast fashioned twice this *Soul* of ours,
So that she is by double title Thine;
Thou only knowest her nature and her pow'rs,
Her subtle form Thou only canst define.                    248

To judge herself she must herself transcend,
As greater circles comprehend the less;
But she wants power, her own powers to extend,
As fettered men cannot their strength express.                    252

But Thou bright Morning Star, Thou rising *Sun*,
Which in these later times hast brought to light
Those mysteries, that since the world begun,
Lay hid in darkness, and eternal night:                    256

Thou (*like the sun*) dost with indifferent ray,
Into the *palace* and the *cottage* shine,
And show'st the *soul* both to the clerk and lay,
By the clear *lamp* of Thy *Oracle* divine.                260

This Lamp through all the regions of my brain,
Where my *soul* sits, doth spread such beams of grace,
As now, me thinks, I do distinguish plain,
Each subtle line of her immortal face.                     264

## What the Soul Is.

*The soul a substance*, and a *spirit* is,
Which *God* Himself doth in the body make;
Which makes the *Man*: for every man from this,
The *nature* of a *Man*, and *name* doth take.             268

And though this spirit be to the body knit,
As an apt mean her powers to exercise;
Which are *life*, *motion*, *sense*, and *will*, and *wit*,
Yet she *survives*, although the body *dies*.               272

## That the Soul is a Thing Subsisting by Itself.

*She is a substance*, and a real thing,
Which hath itself an actual working might;
Which neither from the Senses' power doth spring,
Nor from the body's humors, tempered right.                276

She is a *vine*, which doth no propping need,
To make her spread herself or spring upright;
She is a *star*, whose beams do not proceed
From any *sun*, but from a *native* light.                 280

For when she sorts things *present* with things *past*,
And thereby things to *come* doth oft foresee;
When she doth *doubt* at first, and *choose* at last,
These acts her own, without her body be.                    284

When of the dew, which the *eye* and *ear* do take
From flowers abroad, and bring into the brain,
She doth within both wax and honey make:
This work is hers, this is her proper pain.                 288

When she from sundry acts, one skill doth draw,
Gathering from divers fights one art of war;
From many cases like, one rule of Law;
These her collections, not the *Senses* are.               292

When in th' effects she doth the causes know,
And seeing the stream, thinks where the spring doth rise;
And seeing the branch, conceives the root below;
These things she views without the body's eyes.            296

When she, without a *Pegasus*, doth fly
Swifter than lightning's fire from *East* to *West*,
About the *Center* and above the *sky*,
She travels then, although the body rest.                  300

When all her works she formeth first within,
Proportions them, and sees their perfect end,
Ere she in act doth any part begin;
What instruments doth then the body lend?                  304

When without hands she doth thus *castles* build,
Sees without eyes, and without feet doth run;
When she digests the world, yet is not filled:
By her own power these miracles are done.                  308

When she defines, argues, divides, compounds,
Considers *virtue*, *vice*, and *general things*,
And marrying divers principles and grounds,
Out of their match a true conclusion brings.               312

These actions in her closet all alone,
(Retired within herself) she doth fulfill;
Use of her body's organs she hath none,
When she doth use the powers of Wit and Will.          316

Yet in the body's prison so she lies,
As through the body's windows she must look;
Her divers powers of *sense* to exercise,
By gathering notes out of the *World's* great book.          320

Nor can herself discourse or judge of ought,
But what the *Sense* collects and home doth bring;
And yet the power of her discoursing thought,
From these collections, is a diverse thing.          324

For though our eyes can nought but colors see,
Yet colors give them not their power of sight;
So, though these fruits of *Sense* her objects be,
Yet she discerns them by her proper light.          328

The workman on his stuff his skill doth show,
And yet the stuff gives not the man his skill;
*Kings* their affairs do by their servants know,
But order them by their own royal will.          332

So, though this cunning mistress and this queen,
Doth, as her instrument, the *Senses* use,
To know all things that are *felt*, *heard*, or *seen*,
Yet she herself doth only *judge* and *choose*:          336

Even as our great wise *Empress* that now reigns
By *sovereign* title over sundry Lands;
Borrows in mean affairs her *subjects'* pains,
Sees by their eyes, and writes by their hands;          340

But things of weight and consequence indeed,
Herself doth in her chamber them debate;
Where all her Counselors she doth exceed
As far in judgment, as she doth in State.          344

Or as the man whom she doth now advance,
Upon her gracious *mercy-seat* to sit;
Doth common things, of course and circumstance,
To the reports of common men commit:                    348

But when the cause itself must be decreed,
Himself in person, in his proper Court,
To grave and solemn hearing doth proceed,
Of every proof and every by-report.                     352

Then, like God's angel he pronounceth right,
And milk and honey from his tongue doth flow;
Happy are they that still are in his sight,
To reap the wisdom which his lips do sow.                356

Right so the *Soul*, which is a lady free,
And doth the justice of her *State* maintain;
Because the senses ready servants be,
Attending nigh about her Court, the brain:              360

By them the forms of outward things she learns,
For they return into the fantasy,
What ever each of them abroad discerns,
And there enroll it for the Mind to see.                364

But when she sits to judge the good and ill,
And to discern betwixt the false and true;
She is not guided by the *Senses'* skill,
But doth each thing in her own mirror view.             368

Then she the *Senses* checks, which oft do err,
And even against their false reports decrees;
And oft she doth condemn what they prefer,
For with a power above the *Sense*, she sees.           372

Therefore no *Sense* the precious joys conceives,
Which in her private contemplations be;
For then the ravished spirit the *Senses* leaves,
Hath her own powers, and proper actions free.           376

Her harmonies are sweet, and full of skill,
When on the Body's instrument she plays;
But the proportions of the *wit* and *will*,
Those sweet accords, are even the angel's lays.          380

These tunes of *Reason* are *Amphion's* lyre,
Wherewith he did the *Theban* city found;
These are the notes wherewith the heavenly *quire*,
The praise of Him which made the heaven doth sound.   384

Then her *self-being nature* shines in this,
That she performs her noblest works alone;
"The *work*, the touch-stone of the *nature* is,
"And by their operations, things are known.          388

## That the Soul is more than a Perfection or Reflection of the Sense.

*Are they not senseless* then, that think the Soul
Nought but a fine perfection of the *Sense*;
Or of the forms which *fancy* doth enroll,
A *quick resulting*, and a *consequence*?          392

What is it then that doth the *Sense* accuse,
Both of *false judgements*, and *fond appetites*?
What makes us do what *Sense* doth most refuse?
Which oft in torment of the *Sense* delights?          396

*Sense* thinks the *planets*, *spheres* not much asunder;
What tells us then their distance is so far?
*Sense* thinks the lightning borne before the thunder;
What tells us then they both together are?          400

When men seem crows far off upon a tower,
*Sense* saith, th' are crows; what makes us think them men?
When we in *agues*, think all sweet things sour,
What makes us know our tongue's false judgement then? 404

What power was that, whereby *Medea* saw,
And well approved, and praised the better course,
When her rebellious *Sense* did so withdraw
Her feeble powers, as she pursued the worse?          408

Did *Sense* persuade *Ulysses* not to hear
The mermaid's songs, which so his men did please;
As they were all persuaded, through the ear
To quit the ship, and leap into the *seas*?                              412

Could any power of *Sense* the *Roman move*,
To burn his own right hand with courage stout?
Could *Sense* make *Marius* sit unbound, and prove
The cruel lancing of the knotty gout?                                416

Doubtless in *Man* there is a *nature* found,
Beside the *Senses*, and above them far;
"Though most men being in sensual pleasures drowned,
"It seems their *Souls* but in their *Senses* are.                        420

If we had nought but *Sense*, then only they
Should have sound minds, which have their *Senses* sound;
But *Wisdom* grows, when *Senses* do decay,
And *Folly* most in quickest *Sense* is found.                            424

If we had nought but *Sense*, each living wight,
Which we call *brute*, would be more sharp than we;
As having *Sense's apprehensive might*,
In a more clear, and excellent degree.                              428

But they do want that *quick discoursing power*,
Which doth in us the erring *Sense* correct;
Therefore the *bee* did suck the painted flower,
And *birds*, of grapes, the cunning shadow, pecked.                  432

*Sense* outsides knows; the Soul through al things sees;
*Sense*, *circumstance*; she, doth the *substance* view;
*Sense* sees the bark, but she, the life of trees;
*Sense* hears the sounds, but she, the concords true.                436

But why do I the *Soul* and *Sense* divide?
When *Sense* is but a power, which she extends;
Which being in divers parts diversified,
The divers forms of objects apprehends?                              440

This power spreads outward, but the root doth grow
In th' inward *Soul*, which only doth perceive;
For th' *eyes* and *ears* no more their objects know,
Then glasses know what faces they receive.                    444

For if we chance to fixe our thoughts elsewhere,
Although our eyes be ope, we cannot see;
And if one power did not both see and hear,
Our sights and sounds would always double be.                 448

Then is the *Soul* a nature, which contains
The power of *Sense*, within a greater power
Which doth employ and use the *Senses'* pains,
But sits and rules within her private bower.                  452

## That the Soul is more than the Temperature of the Humors of the Body.

*If she doth then* the subtle *Sense* excel,
How gross are they that drown her in the blood!
Or in the body's humors tempered well,
As if in them such high perfection stood?                     456

As if most skill in that *Musician* were,
Which had the best, and best tuned instrument;
As if the pencil neat and colors clear,
Had power to make the Painter excellent.                      460

Why doth not beauty then refine the wit?
And good complexion rectify the will?
Why doth not health bring wisdom still with it?
Why doth not sickness make men brutish still?                 464

Who can in *memory*, or *wit*, or *will*,
Or *air*, or *fire*, or *earth*, or *water* find?
What alchemist can draw, with all his skill,
The *quintessence* of these, out of the mind?                 468

If th' *elements* which have nor *life*, nor *sense*,
Can breed in us so great a power as this;
Why give they not themselves like excellence,
Or other things wherein their mixture is?　　　　472

If she were but the Body's quality
Then would she be with it *sick*, *maim'd* and *blind*;
But we perceive where these privations be
A *healthy*, *perfect*, and *sharp-sighted* mind.　　　476

If she the body's nature did partake,
Her strength would with the body's strength decay;
But when the body's strongest sinews slake,
Then is the *Soul* most active, quick and gay.　　　480

If she were but the body's accident,
And her sole *being* did in it subsist;
As *white in snow*; she might herself absent,
And in the body's substance not be mist.　　　484

But *it* on *her*, not *she* on *it* depends;
For *she* the body doth sustain and cherish;
Such secret powers of life to it she lends,
That when they fail, then doth the body perish.　　　488

Since then the *Soul works by herself alone*,
*Springs not from Sense, nor humors, well agreeing*;
Her nature is peculiar, and her own:
She is a *substance*, and a *perfect being*.　　　492

### That the Soul is a Spirit.

But though this substance be the root of *Sense*,
*Sense* knows her not, which doth but *bodies* know;
*She is a spirit*, and heavenly influence,
Which from the fountain of God's Spirit doth flow.　　　496

She is a Spirit, yet not like *air*, or *wind*,
Nor like the *spirits* about the *heart* or *brain*;
Nor like those spirits which alchemists do find,
When they in everything seek gold in *vain*.　　　500

For she all *natures* under heaven doth pass;
Being like those spirits, which God's bright face do see;
Or like *Himself*, Whose *image* once she was,
Though now (alas!) she scarce His *shadow* be.          504

Yet of the *forms*, she holds the first degree,
That are to gross material bodies knit;
Yet she herself is *bodiless* and free;
And though confined, is almost infinite.          508

### That It cannot be a Body.

Were she a *body* how could she remain
Within this body, which is less than she?
Or how could she the world's great shape contain,
And in our narrow breasts containèd bee?          512

All *bodies* are confined within some place,
But *she* all place within herself confines;
All *bodies* have their measure, and their space,
But who can draw the *Soul's* dimensive lines?          516

No *body* can at once two forms admit,
Except the one the other do deface;
But in the *soul* ten thousand forms do sit,
And none intrudes into her neighbor's place.          520

All *bodies* are with other bodies filled,
But she receives both heaven and earth together;
Nor are their forms by rash encounter spilled,
For there they stand, and neither toucheth either.          524

Nor can her wide embracements fillèd be;
For they that most, and greatest things embrace,
Enlarge thereby their minds' capacity,
As streams enlarged, enlarged the channel's space.          528

*All things received, do such proportion take,*
*As those things have, wherein they are received*:
So little glasses little faces make,
And narrow webs on narrow frames be weaved;          532

Then what vast body must we make the *mind*
Wherein are men, beasts, trees, towns, seas, and lands;
And yet each thing a proper place doth find,
And each thing in the true proportion stands?          536

Doubtless this could not be, but that she turns
Bodies to spirits, by *sublimation* strange;
As fire converts to fire the things it burns
As we our meats into our nature change.          540

From their gross *matter* she abstracts the *forms*,
And draws a kind of *quintessence* from things;
Which to her proper nature she transforms,
To bear them light on her celestial wings:          544

This doth she, when, from things *particular*,
She doth abstract the *universal kinds*;
Which bodiless and immaterial are,
And can be lodged but only in our minds:          548

And thus from diverse *accidents* and *acts*,
Which do within her observation fall,
She goddesses, and powers divine, abstracts:
As *Nature*, *Fortune*, and the *Virtues* all.          552

Again, how can she several *bodies* know,
If in herself a *body's* form she bear?
How can a mirror sundry faces show,
If from all shapes and forms it be not clear?          556

Nor could we by our eyes all colors learn,
Except our eyes were of all colors void;
Nor sundry tastes can any tongue discern,
Which is with gross and bitter humors cloyed.          560

Nor may a man of *passions* judge aright,
Except his mind be from all passions free;
Nor can a *Judge* his office well acquit,
If he possessed of either party be.          564

If lastly, this quick power a body were,
Were it as swift as is the *wind* or *fire*;
(Whose atomies do th' one down side-ways bear,
And make the other in *pyramids* aspire:)                    568

Her nimble body yet in time must move,
And not in instants through all places slide;
But she is nigh, and far, beneath, above,
In point of time, which thought cannot divide:              572

She is sent as soon to *China* as to *Spain*,
And thence returns, as soon as she is sent;
She measures with one time, and with one pain,
An ell of silk, and heaven's wide spreading tent.          576

As then the *Soul* a substance hath alone,
Besides the Body in which she is confined;
So hath she not a *body* of her own,
But is a *spirit*, and *immaterial mind*.                   580

### That the Soul is Created Immediately by God.

*Since body and soul* have such diversities,
Well might we muse, how first their match began;
But that we learn, that He that spread the skies,
And fixed the Earth, first form'd the *soul* in man.        584

This true *Prometheus* first made Man of earth,
And shed in him a beam of heavenly fire;
Now in their mother's wombs before their birth,
Doth in all sons of men their *souls* inspire.             588

And as *Minerva* is in fables said,
From *Jove*, without a mother to proceed;
So our true *Jove*, without a mother's aid,
Doth daily millions of *Minervas* breed.                   592

### Erroneous Opinions of the Creation of Souls.

Then neither from eternity before,
Nor from the time when *Time's* first point begun;
Made He all *souls*: which now He keeps in store,
Some in the moon, and others in the sun:                    596

Nor in a *secret cloister* doth He keep
These virgin-spirits, until their marriage-day;
Nor locks them up in chambers, where they sleep,
Till they awake, within these beds of clay.                 600

Nor did He first a certain number make,
Infusing part in *beasts*, and part in *men*,
And, as unwilling further pains to take,
Would make no more than those He framèd then.              604

So that the widow *Soul* her *body* dying,
Unto the next-borne *body* married was;
And so by often changing and supplying,
Mens' *souls* to beasts, and beasts to men did pass.       608

(These thoughts are fond;[1] for since the bodies borne
Be more in number far then those that dye;
Thousands must be abortive, and forlorn,
Ere others' deaths to them their *souls* supply.)          612

But as God's *handmaid*, *Nature*, doth create
Bodies in time distinct, and order due;
So God gives *souls* the like successive date,
Which *Himself* makes, in bodies formèd new:               616

Which *Himself* makes, of no material thing;
For unto angels He no power hath given,
Either to form the shape, or stuff to bring
From *air* or *fire*, or *substance of the heaven*.        620

---

1  Foolish

Nor He in this doth *Nature's* service use;
For though from bodies, she can bodies bring,
Yet could she never souls from Souls *traduce*,[2]
As fire from fire, or light from light doth spring.     624

### Objection: That the Soul is Extraduce.

Alas! that some, that were great lights of old,
And in their hands the *lamp* of God did bear;
Some reverend Fathers did this error hold,
Having their eyes dimmed with religious fear!     628

For when (say they) by Rule of Faith we find,
That every *soul* unto her *body* knit,
Brings from the mother's womb, the *sin of kind*,
The root of all the ill she doth commit.     632

How can we say that God the *Soul* doth make,
But we must make Him author of her sin?
Then from man's soul she doth beginning take,
Since in man's soul corruption did begin.     636

For if God make her, first He makes her ill,
(Which God forbid our thoughts should yield unto!)
Or makes the body her fair form to spill,
Which, of itself it had no power to do.     640

Not *Adam's body* but his *soul* did sin,
And so herself unto corruption brought;
But the poor *soul* corrupted is within,
Ere she had sinned, either in act, or thought:     644

And yet we see in her such powers divine,
As we could gladly think, *from God she came*;
Fain would we make Him Author of the wine,
If for the dregs we could some other blame.     648

---

2   To produce as offspring; see OED 3b

65

### The Answer to the Objection.

*Thus these* good men with holy zeal were blind,
When on the other part the truth did shine;
Whereof we do clear demonstrations find,
By light of *Nature*, and by light *Divine*                    652

None are so gross as to contend for this,
That souls from bodies may traducèd be;
Between whose natures no proportion is,
When root and branch in nature still agree.               656

But many subtle wits have justified,
That *souls* from *souls* spiritually may spring;
Which (if the nature of the *soul* be tried)
Will even in Nature prove as gross a thing.               660

### Reasons Drawn from Nature

For all things made, are either made of nought,
Or made of stuff that ready made doth stand;
Of nought no creature ever formèd ought,
For that is proper to th' Almighty's hand.                664

If then the *soul* another *soul* do make,
Because her power is kept within a bound,
She must some former stuff or *matter* take;
But in the soul there is no *matter* found.               668

Then if her heavenly Form do not agree
With any *matter* which the world contains;
Then she of nothing must created bee,
And to *create*, to God alone pertains.                   672

Again, if *souls* do other *souls* beget,
'Tis by themselves, or by the body's power;
If by themselves, what doth their working let,
But they might *souls* engender every hour?               676

If by the body, how can *wit* and *will*
Join with the body only in this act?
Since when they do their other works fulfill,
They from the body do themselves *abstract*?          680

Again, if *souls* of *souls* begotten were,
Into each other they should change and move;
And *change* and *motion still corruption* bear;
How shall we then the *soul* immortal prove?          684

If lastly, *souls* do generation use,
Then should they spread incorruptible seed;
What then becomes of that which they do lose,
When th' acts of generation do not speed?          688

And though the *soul* could cast spiritual seed,
Yet *would* she not, because she *never dies*;
For mortal things desire their *like* to breed,
That so they may their kind immortalize.          692

Therefore the angels, sons of God are nam'd,
And marry not, nor are in marriage given;
Their spirits and ours are of one *substance* framed,
And have one Father, even the *Lord of heaven*:          696

Who would at first, that in each other thing,
The *earth* and *water* living *souls* should breed;
But that *man's soul* whom He would make their king,
Should from Himself immediately proceed.          700

And when He took the *woman* from *man's* side,
Doubtless Himself inspired her *soul* alone;
For 'tis not said, He did *man's soul* divide,
But took *flesh of his flesh, bone of his bone.*          704

Lastly, God being made Man for man's own sake,
And being like Man in all, except in sin,
His body from the *virgin's* womb did take;
But all agree, *God form'd His soul within.*          708

Then is the *soul* from God; so *Pagans* say,
Which saw by *Nature's* light her heavenly kind;
Naming her *kin to God*, and *God's bright ray*,
A citizen of Heaven to Earth confined.                    712

But now, I feel, they pluck me by the ear
Whom my young *Muse* so boldly termèd blind;
And crave more heavenly light, that cloud to clear,
Which makes them think God doth not make the mind.   716

### Reasons Drawn from Divinity.

God doubtless makes her, and doth make her good,
And grafts her in the body, there to spring;
Which, though it be corrupted, flesh and blood
Can no way to the *Soul* corruption bring:                720

And yet this *Soul* (made good by God at first,
And not corrupted by the body's ill)
Even in the womb is sinful, and accursed,
Ere she can *judge* by *wit* or *choose* by *will*.          724

Yet is not God the Author of her sin
Though Author of her *being*, and *being there*;
And if we dare to judge our *Judge* herein,
He can condemn us, and Himself can clear.               728

First, God from infinite eternity
*Decreed*, what *hath been*, *is*, or *shall be* done;
And was resolved, that every man should be,
And in his turn, his race of life should run:            732

And so did purpose all the *souls* to make,
That ever *have been* made, or *ever shall*;
And that their *being* they should only take
In human bodies, or not *be* at all.                     736

Was it then fit that such a weak event
(*Weakness itself*—the sin and fall of Man)
His counsel's execution should prevent,
Decreed and fixed before the World began?                740

Or that one *penal law* by *Adam* broke,
Should make God break His own *eternal Law*;
The settled order of the World revoke,
And change all forms of things, which He foresaw?          744

Could *Eve's weak* hand, extended to the tree,
In sunder rend that ad*amantine chain*,
Whose golden links, *effects* and causes be,
And which to God's own chair doth fixed remain?          748

O could we see, how cause from cause doth spring!
How mutually they linked and folded are!
And hear how oft one disagreeing string
The harmony doth rather make than mar!          752

And view at once, how *death* by *sin* is brought,
And how from *death*, a better *life* doth rise,
How this God's *justice*, and His *mercy* taught:
We this decree would praise, as right and wise.          756

But we that measure times by first and last,
The sight of things successively, do take;
When God on all at once His view doth cast,
And of all times doth but one *instant* make.          760

All in *Himself* as in a *glass* He sees,
For *from Him, by Him, through Him, all things be*:
His sight is not discursive, by degrees,
But seeing the whole, each single part doth see.          764

He looks on *Adam*, as a *root*, or *well*,
And on his heirs, as *branches*, and as *streams*;
He sees *all* men as *one* Man, though they dwell
In sundry cities, and in sundry realms:          768

And as the *root* and *branch* are but one *tree*,
And *well* and *stream* do but one *river* make;
So, if the *root* and *well* corrupted be,
The *stream* and *branch* the same corruption take:          772

So, when the root and fountain of Mankind
Did draw corruption, and God's curse, by sin;
This was a charge that all his heirs did bind,
And all his offspring grew corrupt therein.                776

And as when the hand doth strike, the Man offends,
(For *part from whole, Law severs not in this*)
So *Adam's* sin to the whole kind extends;
For all their natures are but part of his.                 780

Therefore this *sin of kind*, not personal,
But real and hereditary was;
The guilt whereof, and punishment to all,
By course of Nature, and of Law doth pass.                784

For as that easy Law was given to all,
To ancestor and heir, to first and last;
So was the first transgression general,
And all did pluck the fruit and all did taste.            788

Of this we find some footprints in our Law,
Which doth her root from God and Nature take;
Ten thousand men she doth together draw,
And of them all, one Corporation make:                    792

Yet these, and their successors, are but one,
And if they gain or lose their liberties;
They harm, or profit not themselves alone,
But such as in succeeding times shall rise.               796

And so the ancestor, and all his heirs,
Though they in number pass the stars of heaven,
Are still but one; his forfeitures are theirs,
And unto them are his advancements given:                 800

His civil acts do bind and bar them all;
And as from *Adam*, all corruption take,
So, if the father's crime be *capital*
In all the *blood*, Law doth *corruption* make.           804

Is it then just with us, to dis-inherit
The unborn nephews for the father's fault?
And to advance again for one man's merit,
A thousand heirs, that have deservèd nought?          808

And is not God's decree as just as ours,
If He, for *Adam's sin*, his sons deprive,
Of all those native virtues, and those powers,
Which He to him, and to his race did give?          812

For what is this contagious sin of kind
But a privation of that grace within?
And of that great rich dowry of the mind
Which all had had, but for the first man's sin?          816

If then a man, on light conditions gain
A great estate, to him and his, for ever;
If willfully he forfeit it again
Who doth bemoan his heir or blame the giver?          820

So, though God make the *Soul* good, rich and fair,
Yet when her form is to the body knit,
Which makes the Man, which man is *Adam's heir*
Justly forth-with He takes His grace from it:          824

And then the soul being first from nothing brought,
When God's grace fails her, doth to nothing fall;
And this *declining proneness unto nought*,
Is even that sin that we are borne withal.          828

Yet not alone the first good qualities,
Which in the first *soul* were, deprivèd are;
But in their place the contrary do rise,
And real spots of sin her beauty mar.          832

Nor is it strange, that Adam's ill desert
Should be transferred unto his guilty Race;
When Christ His grace and justice doth impart
To men unjust, and such as have no grace.          836

Lastly, the *Soul* were better so to be
Borne slave to sin, then not to be at all;
Since (if she do believe) One sets her free,
That makes her mount the higher for her fall.        840

*Yet this* the curious wits will not content;
They yet will know (since God foresaw this ill)
Why His high Providence did not prevent
The declination of the first man's will.        844

If by His Word He had the current staid
Of *Adam's* will, which was by nature free;
It had been one, as if His Word had said,
I will henceforth that *Man no man shall be.*        848

For what is Man without a moving mind,
Which hath a judging *wit*, and choosing *will*?
Now, if God's power should her election bind,
Her motions then would cease and stand all still.        852

And why did God in man this *soul* infuse,
But that he should his Maker *know* and *love*?
Now, if *love* be compelled and cannot choose,
How can it grateful or thankworthy prove?        856

Love must free-hearted be, and voluntary,
And not enchanted, or by Fate constrained;
Nor like that love, which did *Ulysses* carry,
To *Circe's* isle, with mighty charms enchained.        860

Besides, were we unchangeable in *will*,
And of a *wit* that nothing could mis-deem;
Equal to God, Whose wisdom shineth still,
And never errs, we might ourselves esteem.        864

So that if Man would be invariable,
He must be God, or like a rock or tree;
For even the perfect Angels were not stable,
But had a fall more desperate than we.        868

Then let us praise that Power, which makes us be
*Men* as we are, and rest contented so;
And knowing Man's fall was curiosity,
Admire God's counsels, which we cannot know.          872

And let us know that God the Maker is
Of all the *Souls*, in all the men that be:
Yet their corruption is no fault of His,
But the first man's that broke God's first decree.          876

## Why the Soul is United to the Body.

*This substance*, and this *spirit of God's own making*,
Is in the body placed, and planted here;
"That both of God, and of the world partaking,
"Of all that is, Man might the image bear.          880

God first made angels bodiless, pure minds,
Then other things, which mindless bodies be;
Last, He made Man, th' *horizon* 'twixt both kinds,
In whom we do the World's abridgment see.          884

Besides, this World below did need *one wight*,
Which might thereof distinguish every part;
Make use thereof, and take therein delight,
And order things with industry and art:          888

Which also God might in His works admire,
And here beneath, yield Him both prayer and praise;
As there, above, the holy angels quire
Doth spread His glory with spiritual lays.          892

Lastly, the brute, unreasonable wights,
Did want a *visible king* on them to reign:
And God, Himself thus to the World unites,
That so the World might endless bliss obtain.          896

## In What Manner the Soul is United to the Body.

"But how shall we this *union* well express?
Nought ties the *soul*; her subtlety is such
She moves the body, which she doth possess,
Yet no part touches, but by *Virtue's* touch.                    900

Then dwells she not therein as in a tent,
Nor as a pilot in his ship doth sit;
Nor as the spider in his web is pent;
Nor as the wax retains the print in it;                    904

Nor as a vessel water doth contain;
Nor as one liquor in another shed;
Nor as the heat doth in the fire remain;
Nor as a voice throughout the air is spread:                    908

But as the fair and cheerful *Morning light*,
Doth here and there her silver beams impart,
And in an instant doth herself unite
To the transparent air, in all, and part:                    912

Still resting whole, when blows the air divide;
Abiding pure, when th' air is most corrupted;
Throughout the air, her beams dispersing wide,
And when the air is tossed, not interrupted:                    916

So doth the piercing *Soul* the body fill,
Being all in all, and all in part diffus'd;
Indivisible, incorruptible still,
Not forced, encountered, troubled or confused.                    920

And as the *sun* above, the light doth bring,
Though we behold it in the air below;
So from the Eternal Light the *Soul* doth spring,
Though in the body she her powers do show.                    924

### How the Soul doth Exercise Her Powers in the Body.

*But* as the world's *sun* doth effects beget,
Diverse, in diverse places every day;
Here *Autumn's* temperature, there *Summer's* heat,
Here flow'ry *Spring-tide*, and there *Winter* gray:                    928

Here *Even*, there *Morn*, here *Noon*, there *Day*, there *Night*;
Melts wax, dries clay, makes flowers, some quick, some dead;
Makes the *More* black, and th' *European* white,
Th' *American* tawny, and th' *East-Indian* red:                    932

So in our little World: this *soul* of ours,
Being only one, and to one body tied,
Doth use, on diverse objects diverse powers,
And so are her effects diversified.                    936

### The Vegetative or Quickening Power.

*Her quick'ning* power in every lining part,
Doth as a nurse, or as a mother serve;
And doth employ her *economic* art,
And busy care, her household to preserve                    940

Here she *attracts*, and there she doth *retain*,
There she *decocts*, and doth the food prepare;
There she *distributes* it to every vein,
There she *expels* what she may fitly spare.                    944

This power to *Martha* may comparèd be,
Which busy was, the *household-things* to do;
Or to a *Dryas*, living in a tree:
For even to trees this power is proper too.                    948

And though the Soul may not this power extend
Out of the body, but still use it there;
She hath a power which she abroad doth send,
Which views and searches all things everywhere.                    952

## *The Power of Sense.*

*This power is Sense*, which from abroad doth bring
The *color, taste*, and *touch*, and *scent*, and *sound*;
The *quantity*, and *shape* of every thing
Within th' Earth's center, or Heaven's circle found.        956

This power, in parts made fit, fit objects takes,
Yet not the things, but forms of things receives;
As when a seal in wax impression makes,
The print therein, but not itself it leaves.        960

And though things sensible be numberless,
But only five the *Senses'* organs be;
And in those five, all things their forms express,
Which we can *touch, taste, feel*, or *hear*, or *see*.        964

These are the windows through the which she views
The *light of knowledge*, which is life's loadstar:
"And yet while she these spectacles doth use,
"Oft worldly things seem greater than they are.        968

## *Sight.*

First, the two *eyes* that have the *seeing* power,
Stand as one watchman, spy, or sentinel;
Being placed aloft, within the head's high tower;
And though both see, yet both but one thing tell.        972

These mirrors take into their little space
The forms of *moon* and *sun*, and every *star*;
Of every body and of every place,
Which with the World's wide arms embracèd are:        976

Yet their best object, and their noblest use,
Hereafter in another World will be;
When God in them shall heavenly light infuse,
That face to face they may their *Maker* see.        980

Here are they guides, which do the body lead,
Which else would stumble in eternal night;
Here in this world they do much knowledge *read*,
And are the casements which admit most light:            984

They are her farthest reaching instrument,
Yet they no beams unto their objects send;
But all the rays are from their objects sent,
And in the *eyes* with pointed angles end:            988

If th' objects be far off, the rays do meet
In a sharp point, and so things seem but small;
If they be near, their rays do spread and fleet,
And make broad points, that things seem great withal.   992

Lastly, nine things to *Sight* requirèd are;
The *power* to see, the *light*, the *visible* thing,
Being not too *small*, too *thin*, too *nigh*, too *far*,
*Clear* space, and *time*, the form distinct to bring.            996

Thus we see how the *Soul* doth use the eyes,
As instruments of her quick power of sight;
Hence do th' Arts *optic* and fair *painting* rise:
*Painting*, which doth all gentle minds delight.            1000

### Hearing.

Now let us hear how she the *Ears* employs:
Their office is the troubled air to take,
Which in their mazes forms a sound or noise,
Whereof herself doth true distinction make.            1004

These wickets of the *Soul* are placed on high
Because all sounds do lightly mount aloft;
And that they may not pierce too violently,
They are delayed with turns, and windings oft.            1008

For should the voice directly strike the brain,
It would astonish and confuse it much;
Therefore these plaits and folds the sound restrain,
That it the organ may more gently touch.            1012

As streams, which with their winding banks do play,
Stopped by their creeks, run softly through the plain;
So in the Ears' labyrinth the voice doth stray,
And doth with easy motion touch the brain.                    1016

It is the slowest, yet the daintiest *sense*;
For even the *Ears* of such as have no skill,
Perceive a discord, and conceive offense;
And knowing not what is good, yet find the ill.               1020

And though this *sense* first gentle *Music* found,
Her proper object is *the speech of men*;
But that speech chiefly which God's heralds sound,
When their tongues utter what His Spirit did pen.             1024

Our *Eyes* have lids, our *Ears* still open we see,
Quickly to hear how every tale is provèd;
Our *Eyes* still move, our *Ears* unmovèd be,
That though we hear quick we be not quickly movèd.           1028

Thus by the organs of the *Eye* and *Ear*,
The *Soul* with knowledge doth herself endue;
"Thus she her prison, may with pleasure bear,
"Having such prospects, all the world to view.               1032

These conduit-pipes of knowledge feed the Mind,
But th' other three attend the Body still;
For by their services the *Soul* doth find,
What things are to the body, good or ill.                    1036

## Taste.

The *body's* life with meats and air is fed,
Therefore the *soul* doth use the *tasting* power,
In veins, which through the tongue and palate spread,
Distinguish every relish, sweet and sour.                    1040

This is the body's *nurse*; but since man's wit
Found th' art of *cookery*, to delight his *sense*;
More bodies are consumed and killed with it,
Than with the sword, famine, or pestilence.                  1044

### Smelling.

*Next*, in the nostrils she doth use the *smell*:
As God the *breath of life* in them did give,
So makes He now this power in them to dwell,
To judge all airs, whereby we *breathe* and *live*.        1048

This *sense* is also mistress of an Art,
Which to soft people sweet perfumes doth sell;
Though this dear Art doth little good impart,
"Since they smell best, that do of nothing smell.        1052

And yet good *scents* do purify the brain,
Awake the fancy, and the wits refine;
Hence old *Devotion*, *incense* did ordain
To make mens' spirits apt for thoughts divine.        1056

### Feeling.

*Lastly, the feeling power*, which is Life's root,
Through every living part itself doth shed;
By sinews, which extend from head to foot,
And like a net, all o'er the body spread.        1060

Much like a subtle spider, which doth sit
In middle of her web, which spreadeth wide;
If ought do touch the utmost thread of it,
She feels it instantly on every side.        1064

By *Touch*, the first pure qualities we learn,
Which quicken all things, *hot, cold, moist*, and *dry*;
By *Touch*, *hard, soft, rough, smooth*, we do discern;
By *Touch*, *sweet pleasure*, and *sharp pain*, we try.        1068

These are the outward instruments of Sense,
These are the guards which every thing must pass
Ere it approach the mind's intelligence,
Or touch the Fantasy, *Wit's looking-glass*.        1072

### The Imagination or Common Sense.

And yet these porters, which all things admit,
Themselves perceive not, nor discern the things;
One *common* power doth in the forehead sit,
Which all their proper forms together brings.       1076

For all those *nerves*, which *spirits of Sense* do bear,
And to those outward organs spreading go;
United are, as in a center there,
And there this power those sundry forms doth know.   1080

Those outward organs present things receive,
This inward *Sense* doth absent things retain;
Yet straight transmits all forms she doth perceive,
Unto a higher region of the *brain*.       1084

### The Fantasy.

Where *Fantasy*, near *handmaid* to the mind,
Sits and beholds, and doth discern them all;
Compounds in one, things diverse in their kind;
Compares the black and white, the great and small.   1088

Besides, those single forms she doth esteem,
And in her balance doth their values try;
Where some things good, and some things ill do seem,
And neutral some, in her *fantastic* eye.       1092

This busy power is working day and night;
For when the outward *senses* rest do take,
A thousand dreams, fantastical and light,
With fluttering wings do keep her still awake.       1096

### The Sensitive Memory.

Yet always all may not afore her be;
Successively, she this and that intends;
Therefore such forms as she doth cease to see,
To *Memory's* large volume she commends.       1100

The *ledger-book* lies in the brain behind,
Like *Janus'* eye, which in his poll was set;
The *layman's tables, storehouse of the mind,*
Which doth remember much, and much forget.          1104

Here *Sense's apprehension*, end doth take;
As when a stone is into water cast,
One circle doth another circle make,
Till the last circle touch the bank at last.          1108

## The Passions of Sense.

But though the *apprehensive power* do pause,
The *motive* virtue then begins to move;
Which in the heart below doth PASSIONS cause,
*Joy, grief,* and *fear,* and *hope,* and *hate,* and *love.*          1112

These passions have a free commanding might,
And diverse actions in our life do breed;
For, all acts done without true Reason's light,
Do from the passion of the *Sense* proceed.          1116

But since the *brain* doth lodge the powers of *Sense,*
How makes it in the heart those passions spring?
The mutual love, the kind intelligence
'Twixt heart and brain, this *sympathy* doth bring.          1120

From the kind heat, which in the heart doth reign,
The *spirits* of life do their beginning take;
These *spirits* of life ascending to the brain,
When they come there, the *spirits of Sense* do make.          1124

These *spirits of Sense*, in Fantasy's High Court,
Judge of the forms of *objects*, ill or well;
And so they send a good or ill report
Down to the heart, where all affections dwell.          1128

If the report be *good*, it causeth *love*,
And longing *hope*, and well-assurèd *joy*:
If it be *ill*, then doth it *hatred* move,
And trembling *fear*, and vexing *grief's* annoy.          1132

Yet were these natural affections good:
(For they which want them, *blocks* or *devils* be)
If *Reason* in her first perfection stood,
That she might *Nature's* passions rectify.                    1136

### The Motion of Life.

Besides, another *motive*-power doth rise
Out of the heart; from whose pure blood do spring
The *vital spirits*; which, borne in *arteries*,
Continuous motion to all parts do bring.                       1140

### The Local Motion.

This makes the pulses beat, and lungs respire,
This holds the sinews like a bridle's reins;
And makes the Body to advance, retire,
To turn or stop, as she them slacks, or strains.               1144

Thus the *soul* tunes the *body's* instrument;
These harmonies she makes with *life* and *sense*;
The organs fit are by the body lent,
But th' actions flow from the *Soul's* influence.              1148

### The Intellectual Powers of the Soul.

*But now* I have a *will*, yet want a *wit*,
To express the working of the *wit* and *will*;
Which, though their root be to the body knit,
Use not the body, when they use their skill.                   1152

These powers the nature of the S*oul declare*,
For to man's *soul* these only proper be;
For on the Earth no other wights there are
That have these heavenly powers, but only we.                  1156

### The Wit or Understanding.

The WIT, the pupil of the *Soul's* clear eye,
And in man's world, the only shining *star*;
Looks in the mirror of the Fantasy,
Where all the gatherings of the *Senses* are.               1160

From thence this power the shapes of things abstracts,
And them within her *passive part* receives;
Which are enlightened by that part which *acts*,
And so the forms of single things perceives.               1164

But after, by discoursing to and fro,
Anticipating, and comparing things;
She doth all universal natures know,
And all *effects* into their *causes* brings.               1168

### Reason, Understanding.

When she *rates* things and moves from ground to ground,
The name of *Reason* she obtains by this;
But when by Reason she the truth hath found,
And *standeth fixed*, she UNDERSTANDING is.               1172

### Opinion, Judgement.

When her assent she *lightly* doth incline
To either part, she is OPINION light:
But when she doth by principles define
A certain truth, she hath *true Judgement's* sight.               1176

And as from *Senses*, *Reason's work* doth spring,
So many *reasons understanding* gain;
And many *understandings*, *knowledge* bring;
And by much *knowledge*, *wisdom* we obtain.               1180

So, many stairs we must ascend upright
Ere we attain to *Wisdom's* high degree;
So doth this Earth eclipse our Reason's light.
Which else (in instants) would like angels see.               1184

Yet hath the *Soul* a dowry natural,
And *sparks of light*, some common things to see;
Not being a *blank* where nought is writ at all,
But what the writer will, may written be                                    1188

For Nature in man's heart her laws doth pen;
Prescribing *truth* to *wit*, and *good* to *will*;
Which do *accuse*, or else *excuse* all men,
For every thought or practice, good or ill:                                 1192

And yet these sparks grow almost infinite,
Making the World, and all therein their food;
As fire so spreads as no place holdeth it,
Being nourished still, with new supplies of wood.                          1196

And though these sparks were almost quenched with sin,
Yet they whom that *Just One* hath justified;
Have them increased with heavenly light within,
And like the *widow's oil* still multiplied.                               1200

### The Power of Will.

And as this *wit* should goodness truly know,
We have a *Will*, which that true good should choose;
Though *Will* do oft (when *wit* false forms doth show)
Take *ill* for *good*, and *good* for *ill* refuse.                        1204

### The Relations Betwixt Wit and Will.

*Will* puts in practice what the *Wit* deviseth:
*Will* ever acts, and *Wit* contemplates still;
And as from *Wit*, the power of *wisdom* riseth,
*All other virtues* daughters are of *Will*.                              1208

*Will* is the prince, and *Wit* the counsellor,
Which doth for common good in Council sit;
And when *Wit* is resolved, *Will* lends her power
To execute what is advised by *Wit*.                                       1212

*Wit* is the mind's chief judge, which doth control
Of *Fancy's* Court the judgements, false and vain;
*Will* holds the royal scepter in the *soul*
And on the passions of the heart doth reign.          1216

*Will* is as free as any emperor,
Nought can restrain her *gentle* liberty;
No tyrant, nor no torment, hath the power,
To make us *will*, when we unwilling be.          1220

## The Intellectual Memory.

To these high powers, a store-house doth pertain,
Where they all arts and general reasons lay;
Which in the *Soul*, even after death, remain
And no *Lethaean* flood can wash away.          1224

This is the *Soul*, and these her virtues be;
Which, though they have their sundry proper ends,
And one exceeds another in degree,
Yet each on other mutually depends.          1228

*Our Wit* is given, *Almighty God* to *know*;
*Our Will* is given to *love* Him, being *known*;
But God could not be *known* to us below,
But by His *works* which through the sense are shown.          1232

And as the *Wit* doth reap the fruits of *Sense*,
So doth the *quickening* power the *senses feed*;
Thus while they do their sundry gifts dispense,
The best, the service of the least doth need.          1236

Even so the King his Magistrates do serve,
Yet Commons feed both magistrate and king;
The Commons' peace the magistrates preserve
By borrowed power, which from the Prince doth spring.          1240

The *quickening power* would *be*, and so would rest;
The *Sense* would not *be* only, but *be well*;
But *Wit's* ambition longeth to the *best*,
For it desires in endless bliss to dwell.          1244

And these three powers, three sorts of men do make:
For some, like plants, their veins do only fill;
And some, like beasts, their senses' pleasure take;
And some, like angels, do contemplate still.                    1248

Therefore the fables turned some men to flowers,
And others, did with brutal forms invest;
And did of others, make celestial powers,
Like angels, which still travel, yet still rest.                1252

Yet these three powers are not three *souls*, but one;
As one and two are both contained in *three*;
*Three* being one number by itself alone:
A shadow of the blessed Trinity.                                1256

### An Acclamation.

O! what is Man (great Maker of mankind!)
That Thou to him so great respect dost bear!
That Thou adorn'st him with so bright a mind,
Mak'st him a king, and even an angel's peer!                    1260

O! what a lively life, what heavenly power,
What spreading virtue, what a sparkling fire!
How great, how plentiful, how rich a dower
Dost Thou within this dying flesh inspire!                      1264

Thou leav'st Thy print in other works of Thine,
But Thy whole image Thou in Man hast writ;
There cannot be a creature more divine,
Except (like Thee) it should be infinite.                      1268

But it exceeds man's thought, to think how high
*God* hath raised *Man*, since *God a man* became;
The angels do admire this *Mystery*,
And are astonished when they view the same.                     1272

## *That the Soul is Immortal, and Cannot Die.*

Nor hath He given these blessings for a day,
Nor made them on the body's life depend;
The *Soul* though made in time, *survives for aye*,
And though it hath beginning, sees no end.          1276

Her only *end*, is n*ever-ending* bliss;
Which is, *the eternal face of God to see*;
Who *Last of Ends*, and *First of Causes*, is:
And to do this, she must *eternal* be.          1280

How senseless then, and dead a soul hath he,
Which *thinks* his *soul* doth with his body die!
Or *thinks* not so, but so would have it be,
That he might sin with more security.          1284

For though these light and vicious persons say,
Our *Soul* is but a smoke, or airy blast;
Which, during life, doth in our nostrils play,
And when we die, doth turn to wind at last:          1288

Although they say, *'Come let us eat and drink'*;
Our life is but a spark, which quickly dies;
Though thus they *say*, they know not what to think,
But in their minds ten thousand doubts arise.          1292

Therefore no heretics desire to spread
Their light opinions, like these *Epicures*:
For so the staggering thoughts are comfortèd,
And other men's assent their doubt assures.          1296

Yet though these men against their conscience strive,
There are some sparkles in their flinty breasts
Which cannot be extinct, but still revive;
That though they would, they cannot quite be *beasts*;          1300

But who so makes a mirror of his mind,
And doth with patience view himself therein,
His *Soul's* eternity shall clearly find,
Though the other beauties be defaced with sin.          1304

### Reason I: Drawn from Desire of Knowledge.

First *in Man's mind* we find an appetite
To *learn* and *know the truth* of every thing;
Which is co-natural, and borne with it,
And from the *essence* of the *soul* doth spring.          1308

With this *desire*, she hath a native *might*
To find out every truth, if she had time;
Th' innumerable effects to sort aright,
And by degrees, from cause to cause to climb.          1312

But since our life so fast away doth slide,
As doth a hungry eagle through the wind,
Or as a ship transported with the tide;
Which in their passage leave no print behind;          1316

Of which swift little time so much we spend,
While some few things we through the sense do strain;
That our short race of life is at an end,
Ere we the principles of skill attain.          1320

Or God (which to vain ends hath nothing done)
In vain this *appetite* and *power* hath given;
Or else our knowledge, which is here begun,
Hereafter must be perfected in heaven.          1324

God never gave a *power* to one whole kind,
But most part of that kind did use the same;
Most eyes have perfect sight, though some be blind;
Most legs can nimbly run, though some be lame:          1328

But in this life no *soul* the truth can know
So perfectly, as it hath power to doe;
If then perfection be not found below,
A higher place must make her mount thereto.          1332

### Reason II: Drawn from the Motion of the Soul.

*Again* how can she but immortal be?
When with the motions of both *Will* and *Wit*,
She still aspireth to eternity,
And never rests, till she attain to it?                    1336

Water in conduit pipes, can rise no higher
Then the well-head, from whence it first doth spring:
Then since to eternal GOD she doth aspire,
She cannot be but an eternal thing.                    1340

All moving things to other things do move,
Of the same kind, which shows their nature such;
So *earth* falls down and *fire* doth mount above,
Till both their proper elements do touch.                    1344

### The Soul Compared to a River.

*And as* the moisture, which the thirsty earth
Sucks from the sea, to fill her empty veins,
From out her womb at last doth take a birth,
And runs a *Nymph* along the grassy plains:                    1348

Long doth she stay, as loth to leave the land,
From whose soft side she first did issue make;
She tastes all places, turns to every hand,
Her flow'ry banks unwilling to forsake:                    1352

Yet *Nature* so her streams doth lead and carry,
As that her course doth make no final stay,
Till she herself unto the *Ocean* marry,
Within whose watery bosom first she lay:                    1356

Even so the *Soul* which in this earthly mold
The Spirit of God doth secretly infuse;
Because at first she doth the earth behold,
And only this material world she views:                    1360

At first her *mother-earth* she holdeth dear,
And doth embrace the world and worldly things:
She flies close by the ground, and hovers here,
And mounts not up with her celestial wings.                    1364

Yet under heaven she cannot light on ought
That with her heavenly *nature* doth agree;
She cannot rest, she cannot fix her thought,
She cannot in this world contented be:                         1368

For who did ever yet, in *honor, wealth,*
Or *pleasure of the sense,* contentment find?
Who ever ceased to wish, when he had *health*?
Or having *wisdom* was not vexed in mind?                      1372

Then as a *bee* which among weeds doth fall,
Which seem sweet flowers, with luster fresh and gay;
She lights on that, and this, and tasteth all,
But pleased with none, doth rise, and soar away;              1376

So, when the *Soul* finds here no true content,
And, like *Noah's* dove, can no sure footing take;
She doth return from whence she first was sent,
And flies to *Him* that first her wings did make.             1380

*Wit,* seeking *Truth,* from cause to cause ascends,
And never rests, till it the *first* attain:
*Will,* seeking *Good,* finds many middle ends,
But never stays, till it the *last* do gain.                  1384

Now God, the *Truth,* and *First of Causes* is:
God is the *Last Good End,* which lasteth still;
Being *Alpha* and *Omega* named for this;
*Alpha* to *Wit, Omega* to the *Will.*                        1388

Since then her heavenly kind she doth bewray,
In that to God she doth directly move;
And on no mortal thing can make her stay,
She cannot be from hence, but from above.                     1392

And yet this *First True Cause*, and *Last Good End*,
She cannot here so *well* and *truly* see;
For this perfection she must yet attend,
Till to her *Maker* she espousèd be.                          1396

As a *king's* daughter, being in person sought
Of diverse princes, who do neighbor near;
On none of them can fix a constant thought,
Though she to all do lend a gentle ear:                       1400

Yet she can love a foreign emperor,
Whom of great worth and power she hears to be;
If she be woo'd but by *ambassador*,
Or but his *letters*, or his pictures see:                    1404

For well she knows, that when she shall be brought
Into the *kingdom* where her *Spouse* doth reign;
Her eyes shall see what she conceived in thought,
Himself, his state, his glory, and his train.                 1408

So while the *virgin Soul* on *Earth* doth stay,
She woo'd and tempted is ten thousand ways,
By these great powers, which on the *Earth* bear sway;
The *wisdom of the World*, *wealth*, *pleasure*, *praise*:    1412

With these sometime she doth her time beguile,
These do by fits her Fantasy possess;
But she distastes them all within a while,
And in the sweetest finds a tediousness.                      1416

But if upon the World's Almighty King
She once do fixe her humble loving thought;
Who by His *picture*, drawn in every thing,
And *sacred messages*, her *love* hath sought;               1420

Of Him she thinks, she cannot think too much;
This honey tasted still, is ever sweet;
The pleasure of her ravished thought is such,
As almost here, she with her bliss doth meet:                1424

But when in Heaven she shall His *Essence* see,
This is her *sovereign good, and perfect bliss*:
Her longings, wishings, hopes all finished be,
Her joys are full, her motions rest in this:        1428

There is she crowned with garlands of *content*,
There doth she manna eat, and nectar drink;
That Presence doth such high delights present,
As never tongue could speak, nor heart could think.    1432

## Reason III: From Contempt of Death in the Better Sort of Spirits.

*For this* the better *Souls* do oft despise
The body's death, and do it oft desire;
For when on ground, the burdened balance lies
The empty part is lifted up the higher:        1436

But if the body's death the *soul* should kill,
Then death must needs *against her nature* be;
And were it so, all *souls* would flee it still,
For Nature hates and shuns her contrary.        1440

For all things else, which Nature makes to be,
Their *being* to preserve, are chiefly taught;
And though some things desire a change to see,
Yet never thing did long to turn to nought.        1444

If then by death the *soul* were quenchèd quite,
She could not thus against her nature run;
Since every senseless thing, by Nature's light,
Doth preservation seek, destruction shun.        1448

Nor could the World's best spirits so much err,
If death took all—that they should all agree,
Before this life, their *honor* to prefer;
For what is praise to things that nothing be?        1452

Again, if by the body's prop she stand;
If on the body's life, her life depend;
As *Meleager's* on the fatal brand—
The body's good she only would intend:        1456

We should not find her half so brave and bold,
To lead it to the Wars and to the seas;
To make it suffer watchings, hunger, cold,
When it might feed with plenty, rest with ease.                    1460

Doubtless all *Souls* have a surviving thought;
Therefore of death we think with quiet mind;
But if we think of *being turned to nought*,
A trembling horror in our *souls* we find.                        1464

### Reason IV: From the Fear of Death in the Wicked Souls.

*And as* the better spirit, when she doth bear
A scorn of death, doth show she cannot die;
So when the wicked *Soul* Death's face doth fear,
Even then she proves her own eternity.                            1468

For when Death's form appears, she feareth not
An utter quenching or extinguishment;
She would be glad to meet with such a lot,
That so she might all future ill prevent:                         1472

But she doth doubt what after may befall;
For Nature's law accuseth her within;
And saith, 'Tis true that is affirmed by all,
*That after death there is a pain for sin.*                       1476

Then she which hath been hood-winked from her birth,
Doth first herself within Death's mirror see;
And when her body doth return to earth,
She first takes care, how she alone shall be.                     1480

Who ever sees these irreligious men,
With burden of a sickness weak and faint;
But hears them talking of Religion then,
And vowing of their *souls* to every saint?                       1484

When was there ever cursèd *atheist* brought
Unto the *gibbet*, but he did adore
That blessed Power, which he had set at nought,
Scorned and blasphemèd all his life before?                       1488

These light vain persons still are drunk and mad,
With surfeitings and pleasures of their youth;
But at their deaths they are fresh, sober, sad
Then they discern, and then they speak the truth.        1492

If then all *Souls*, both good and bad, do teach,
With general voice, that *souls* can never die;
'Tis not man's flattering gloss, but *Nature's speech*,
Which, like *God's* Oracle, can never lie.               1496

### *Reason V: From the Beneficial Desire of Immortality.*

*Hence springs* that universal strong desire,
Which all men have of Immortality:
Not some few spirits unto this thought aspire,
But all men's minds in this united be.                   1500

Then this desire of Nature is not vain,
She covets not impossibilities;
Fond thoughts may fall into some idle brain,
But one *assent* of all, is ever wise.                   1504

From hence that general care and study springs,
That *launching* and *progression of the mind*;
Which all men have so much, of future things,
That they no joy do in the present find.                 1508

From this desire, that main desire proceeds,
Which all men have surviving Fame to gain;
By *tombs*, by *books*, by *memorable deeds*:
For she that this desires, doth still remain.            1512

Hence lastly, springs care of posterities,
For things their kind would everlasting make;
Hence is it that old men do plant young trees,
The fruit whereof another age shall take.                1516

If we these rules unto ourselves apply,
And view them by reflection of the mind;
All these true notes of immortality
In our *heart's tables* we shall written find.           1520

## Reason VI: From the Very Doubt and Disputation of Immortality.

*And though* some impious wits do questions move,
And doubt if *Souls* immortal be, or no;
That *doubt* their immortality doth prove,
Because they seem immortal things to know.          1524

For he which reasons on both parts doth bring,
Doth some things mortal, some immortal call;
Now, if himself were but a mortal thing,
He could not judge immortal things at all.          1528

For when we judge, our minds we mirrors make:
And as those glasses which material be,
Forms of material things do only take,
For *thoughts* or *minds* in them we cannot see;          1532

So, when we God and angels do conceive,
And think of *truth*, which is eternal too;
Then do our minds immortal forms receive,
Which if they mortal were, they could not do:          1536

And as, if beasts conceived what Reason were,
And that conception should distinctly show,
They should the name of *reasonable* bear;
For without *Reason*, none could *Reason* know:          1540

So when the *Soul* mounts with so high a wing,
As of eternal things she *doubts* can move;
She proofs of her eternity doth bring,
Even when she strives the contrary to prove.          1544

For even the *thought* of immortality,
Being an act done without the body's aid;
Shows, that herself alone could move and be,
Although the body in the grave were laid.          1548

### That the Soul Cannot be Destroyed.

And if herself she can so lively move,
And never need a foreign help to take;
Then must her motion everlasting prove,
Because herself she never can forsake.                        1552


### Her Cause Ceaseth Not.

*But though* corruption cannot touch the mind,
By any cause that from itself may spring;
Some outward cause Fate hath perhaps designed,
Which to the *Soul* may utter quenching bring.               1556


### She hath no Contrary.

*Perhaps* her cause may cease, and she may die;
God is her *cause*, His *Word* her Maker was;
Which shall stand fixed for all eternity
When Heaven and Earth shall like a shadow pass.             1560

*Perhaps* some thing repugnant to her kind,
By strong *antipathy*, the *Soul* may kill;
But what can be *contrary* to the mind,
Which holds all *contraries* in concord still?             1564

She lodgeth heat, and cold, and moist, and dry,
And life, and death, and peace, and war together;
Ten thousand fighting things in her do lie,
Yet neither troubleth, or disturbeth either.                1568


### She Cannot Die for Want of Food.

*Perhaps* for want of food the *soul* may pine;
But that were strange, since all things *bad* and *good*,
Since all God's creatures *mortal* and *divine*,
Since *God Himself*, is her eternal food.                    1572

96

Bodies are fed with things of mortal kind,
And so are subject to mortality;
But *Truth* which is eternal, feeds the mind;
The *Tree of life*, which will not let her die.               1576

### Violence Cannot Destroy Her.

*Yet violence*, perhaps the *Soul* destroys:
As lightning, or the *sun-beams* dim the sight;
Or as a thunder-clap, or cannons' noise,
The power of hearing doth astonish quite.               1580

But high perfection to the *Soul* it brings,
T' encounter things most excellent and high;
For, when she views the best and greatest things
They do not hurt, but rather clear her eye,               1584

Besides—as *Homer's gods* 'gainst armies stand—
Her subtle form can through all dangers slide;
*Bodies are captive*, *minds* endure no band,
And Will is free, and can no force abide.               1588

### Time Cannot Destroy Her.

*But lastly, Time* perhaps at last hath power
To spend her lively powers, and quench her light;
But old god *Saturn* which doth all devour,
Doth cherish her, and still augment her might.               1592

Heaven waxeth old, and all the *spheres* above
Shall one day faint, and their swift motion stay;
And *Time* itself in time shall cease to move;
*Only the Soul survives*, and lives for aye.               1596

Our Bodies, every footstep that they make,
March towards death, until at last they die;
Whether we work, or play, or sleep, or wake,
Our life doth pass, and with *Time's* wings doth fly:               1600

But to the *Soul* Time doth perfection give,
And adds fresh luster to her beauty still;
And makes her in eternal youth to live,
Like her which nectar to the gods doth fill.          1604

The more she lives, the more she feeds on *Truth*;
The more she feeds, her *strength* doth more increase:
And what is *strength*, but an effect of *youth*?
Which if *Time* nurse, how can it ever cease?          1608

## Objections Against the Immortality of the Soul.

*But now* these *Epicures* begin to smile,
And say, my doctrine is more false than true;
And that I fondly do myself beguile,
While these received opinions I ensue.          1612

## Objection I.

For what, say they, doth not the *Soul* wax old?
How comes it then that agèd men do dote;
And that their brains grow sottish, dull and cold,
Which were in youth the only spirits of note?          1616

What? are not *Souls* within themselves corrupted?
How can there idiots then by nature be?
How is it that some wits are interrupted,
That now they dazzled are, now clearly see?          1620

## Answer.

*These questions* make a subtle argument,
To such as think both *sense* and *reason* one;
To whom nor agent, from the instrument,
Nor power of working, from the work is known.          1624

But they that know that wit can show no skill,
But when she things in *Sense's glass* doth view;
Do know, if accident this glass do spill,
It *nothing sees*, or *sees the false for true*.                    1628

For, if that region of the tender brain,
Where th' inward sense of Fantasy should sit,
And the outward senses gatherings should retain,
By Nature, or by chance, become unfit;                    1632

Either at first incapable it is,
And so few things, or none at all receives;
Or marred by accident, which haps amiss
And so amiss it everything perceives.                    1636

Then, as a cunning prince that useth *spies*,
If they return no news doth nothing know;
But if they make advertisement of lies,
The Prince's Counsel all awry do go.                    1640

Even so the *Soul* to such a body knit,
Whose inward senses undisposèd be,
And to receive the forms of things unfit;
Where nothing is brought in, can nothing see.                    1644

This makes the idiot, which hath yet a mind,
Able to *know* the truth, and *choose* the good;
If she such figures in the brain did find,
As might be found, if it in temper stood.                    1648

But if a *frenzy* do possess the brain,
It so disturbs and blots the forms of things;
As Fantasy proves altogether vain,
And to the Wit no true relation brings.                    1652

Then doth the Wit, admitting all for true,
Build fond conclusions on those idle grounds;
Then doth it flee the good, and ill pursue,
Believing all that this false *spy* propounds.                    1656

But purge the humors, and the rage appease,
Which this distemper in the fancy wrought;
Then shall the *Wit*, which never had disease,
Discourse, and judge discreetly, as it ought.        1660

So, though the clouds eclipse the *sun's* fair light,
Yet from his face they do not take one beam;
So have our eyes their perfect power of sight,
Even when they look into a troubled stream.        1664

Then these defects in *Senses'* organs be,
Not in the *soul* or in her working might;
She cannot lose her perfect power to see,
Though mists and clouds do choke her window light.        1668

These imperfections then we must impute,
Not to the agent but the instrument;
We must not blame *Apollo*, but his lute,
If false accords from her false strings be sent.        1672

The *Soul* in all hath one intelligence;
Though too much moisture in an infant's brain,
And too much dryness in an old man's sense,
Cannot the prints of outward things retain:        1676

Then doth the *Soul* want work, and idle sit,
And this we *childishness* and *dotage* call;
Yet hath she then a quick and active Wit,
If she had stuff and tools to work withal:        1680

For, give her organs fit, and objects faire;
Give but the aged man, the young man's sense;
Let but *Medea*, *Aeson's* youth repair,
And straight she shows her wonted excellence.        1684

As a good harper stricken far in years,
Into whose cunning hand the gout is fall;
All his old crotchets in his brain he bears,
But on his harp plays ill, or not at all.        1688

But if *Apollo* takes his gout away,
That he his nimble fingers may apply;
*Apollo's* self will envy at his play,
And all the world applaud his minstrelsy.                    1692

Then *dotage* is no weakness of the mind,
But of the *Sense*; for if the mind did waste,
In all old men we should this wasting find,
When they some certain term of years had past:              1696

But most of them, even to their dying hour,
Retain a mind more lively, quick, and strong;
And better use their understanding power,
Then when their brains were warm, and limbs were young.     1700

For, though the body wasted be and weak,
And though the leaden form of earth it bears;
Yet when we hear that half-dead body speak,
We oft are ravished to the heavenly *spheres*.              1704

## Objection II.

Yet say these men, If all her organs die,
Then hath the *soul* no power her powers to use;
So, in a sort, her powers extinct do lie,
When unto *act* she cannot them reduce.                     1708

And if her powers be dead, then what is she?
For since from every thing some powers do spring,
And from those powers, some *acts* proceeding be,
Then kill both *power* and *act*, and kill the *thing*.     1712

## Answer.

*Doubtless* the body's death when once it dies,
The instruments of sense and life doth kill;
So that she cannot use those faculties,
Although their root rest in her substance still.            1716

But (as the body living) *Wit* and *Will*
Can *judge* and *choose*, without the body's aid;
Though on such objects they are working still,
As through the body's organs are conveyed:                    1720

So, when the body serves her turn no more,
And all her Senses are extinct and gone,
She can discourse of what she learned before,
In heavenly contemplations, all alone.                       1724

So, if one man well on a lute doth play,
And have good horsemanship, and Learning's skill;
Though both his lute and horse we take away,
Doth he not keep his former learning still?                  1728

He keeps it doubtless, and can use it too;
And doth both th' other *skills* in power retain;
And can of both the proper actions doe,
If with his lute or horse he meet again.                     1732

So (though the instruments by which we live,
And view the world, the body's death do kill;)
Yet with the body they shall all revive,
And all their wonted offices fulfill.                        1736

### Objection III.

*But how*, till then, shall she herself employ?
Her spies are dead which brought home news before;
What she hath got and keeps, she may enjoy,
But she hath means to understand no more.                    1740

Then what do those poor *souls*, which nothing get?
Or what do those which get, and cannot keep?
Like buckets bottomless, which all out-let
Those *Souls*, for want of exercise, must sleep.             1744

### Answer.

*See how* man's *Soul* against itself doth strive:
Why should we not have other means to know?
As children while within the womb they live,
Feed by the navel: here they feed not so.                          1748

These children, if they had some use of sense,
And should by chance their mothers' talking hear;
That in short time they shall come forth from thence,
Would fear their birth more than our death we fear.        1752

They would cry out, 'If we this place shall leave,
Then shall we break our tender navel strings;
How shall we then our nourishment receive,
Since our sweet food no other conduit brings?'              1756

And if a man should to these babes reply,
That into this fair world they shall be brought;
Where they shall see the Earth, the Sea, the Sky,
The glorious Sun, and all that God hath wrought:          1760

That there ten thousand dainties they shall meet,
Which by their mouths they shall with pleasure take;
Which shall be cordial too, as well as sweet,
And of their little limbs, tall bodies make:                    1764

This would they think a fable, even as we
Do think the *story* of the *Golden Age*;
Or as some sensual spirits amongst us be,
Which hold the *world to come, a fainèd stage*:            1768

Yet shall these infants after find all true,
Though then thereof they nothing could conceive;
As soon as they are borne, the world they view,
And with their mouths, the nurses'-milk receive.          1772

So, when the *Soul* is borne (for Death is nought
But the *Soul's* birth, and so we should it call)
Ten thousand things she sees beyond her thought,
And in an unknown manner knows them all.                  1776

Then doth she see by spectacles no more,
She hears not by report of double spies;
Herself in instants doth all things explore,
For each thing present, and before her, lies.                    1780

## Objection IV.

*But still* this crew with questions me pursues:
If *souls* deceased (say they) still living be;
Why do they not return, to bring us news
Of that strange world, where they such wonders see?      1784

## Answer.

*Fond men!* If we believe that men do live
Under the *Zenith* of both frozen *Poles*,
Though none come thence advertisement to give;
Why bear we not the like faith of our *souls*?                1788

The *soul* hath here on Earth no more to do,
Then we have business in our mother's womb;
What child doth covet to return thereto?
Although all children first from thence do come?         1792

But as *Noah's* pigeon, which returned no more,
Did show, she footing found, for all the Flood;
So when good souls, departed through Death's door,
Come not again, it shows their dwelling good.             1796

And doubtless, such a *soul* as up doth mount,
And doth appear before her Maker's Face;
Holds this vile world in such a base account,
As she looks down, and scorns this wretched place.       1800

But such as are detruded³ down to Hell,
Either for shame, they still themselves retire;
Or tied in chains, they in close prison dwell,
And cannot come, although they much desire.              1804

---

3   To thrust down

104

## Objection V.

*Well, well,* say these vain spirits, though vain it is
To think our *Souls* to Heaven or Hell to go,
*Politic* men have thought it not amiss,
To spread this *lie,* to make men virtuous so.          1808

## Answer.

*Do you* then think this *moral virtue* good?
I think you do, even for your private gain;
For Commonwealths by *virtue* ever stood,
And common good the private doth contain.          1812

If then this *virtue* you do love so well,
Have you no means, her practice to maintain;
But you this lie must to the people tell,
That good *Souls* live in joy, and ill in pain?          1816

Must *virtue* be preservèd by a *lie?*
*Virtue* and *Truth* do ever best agree;
By this it seems to be a verity,
Since the effects so good and virtuous be.          1820

For, as the devil father is of lies,
So vice and mischief do his lies ensue;
Then this good doctrine did not he devise,
But made this *lie,* which saith it is not true.          1824

## The General Consent of All.

*For how* can that be false, which every tongue
Of every mortal man affirms for true?
Which truth hath in all ages been so strong,
As lodestone-like, all hearts it ever drew.          1828

For, not the *Christian,* or the *Jew* alone,
The *Persian,* or the *Turk,* acknowledge this;
This mystery to the wild *Indian* known,
And to the *Cannibal* and *Tartar* is.          1832

This rich *Assyrian* drug grows everywhere;
As common in the *North*, as in the *East*;
This doctrine does not enter by the *ear*,
But of itself is native in the breast.                    1836

None that acknowledge God, or providence,
Their *Soul's* eternity did ever doubt;
For all *Religion* takes her root from hence,
Which no poor naked nation lives without.                 1840

For since the World for Man created was,
(For only Man the use thereof doth know)
If man do perish like a withered grass,
How doth God's Wisdom order things below?                 1844

And if that Wisdom still wise ends propound,
Why made He man, of other creatures King?
When (if he perish here) there is not found
In all the world so poor and vile a thing?               1848

If death do quench us quite, we have great wrong,
Since for our service all things else were wrought;
That *daws*, and *trees*, and *rocks*, should last so long,
When we must in an instant pass to nought.               1852

But blest be that *Great Power*, that hath us blest
With longer life than Heaven or Earth can have;
Which hath infused into our mortal breast
Immortal powers, not subject to the grave.               1856

For though the Soul do seem her grave to bear,
And in this world is almost buried quick;
We have no cause the body's death to fear,
For when the shell is broke, out comes a chick.          1860

## *Three Kinds of Life Answerable to the Three Powers of the Soul.*

*For* as the *soul's essential* powers are three,
The *quickening power*, the *power of sense* and *reason*;
Three kinds of life to her designèd be,
Which perfect these three powers in their due season.     1864

The first life, in the mother's womb is spent,
Where she her *nursing power* doth only use;
Where, when she finds defect of nourishment,
Sh' expels her body, and this world she views.                    1868

This we call *Birth*; but if the child could speak,
He *Death* would call it; and of Nature plain,
That she would thrust him out naked and weak,
And in his passage pinch him with such pain.                    1872

Yet, out he comes, and in this world is placed,
Where all his *Senses* in perfection be;
Where he finds flowers to smell, and fruits to taste;
And sounds to hear, and sundry forms to see.                    1876

When he hath past some time upon this stage,
His *Reason* then a little seems to wake;
Which, though she spring, when sense doth fade with age,
Yet can she here no perfect practice make.                    1880

Then doth th' aspiring *Soul* the body leave,
Which we call *Death*; but were it known to all,
What *life* our *souls* do by this *death* receive,
Men would it *birth* or *jail-delivery* call.                    1884

In this third life, Reason will be so bright,
As that her spark will like the sun-beams shine;
And shall of God enjoy the real sight.
Being still increased by influence divine.                    1888

## An Acclamation.

O Ignorant poor man! what dost thou bear
Locked up within the casket of thy breast?
What jewels, and what riches hast thou there!
What heavenly treasure in so weak a chest!                    1892

Look in thy *soul*, and thou shalt *beauties* find,
Like those which drowned *Narcissus* in the flood:
*Honor* and *Pleasure* both are in thy mind,
And all that in the world is counted *Good*.                    1896

Think of her worth, and think that God did mean,
This worthy mind should worthy things embrace;
Blot not her beauties with thy thoughts unclean,
Nor her dishonor with thy passions base;                    1900

Kill not her *quickening power* with surfeitings,
Mar not her *Sense* with sensuality;
Cast not her serious wit on idle things:
Make not her free-*will*, slave to vanity.                  1904

And when thou thinks of her *eternity*,
Think not that *Death* against her nature is,
Think it a *birth*; and when thou go to die,
Sing like a swan, as if thou went to bliss.                 1908

And if thou, like a child, didst fear before,
Being in the dark, where thou didst nothing see;
Now I have brought the *torch-light*, fear no more;
Now when thou die, thou canst not hood-winked be.           1912

And thou my *Soul*, which turns thy curious eye,
To view the beams of thine own form divine;
Know, that thou canst know nothing perfectly,
While thou art clouded with this flesh of mine.             1916

Take heed of *overweening*, and compare
Thy peacock's feet with thy gay peacock's train;
Study the best, and highest things that are,
But of thyself a humble thought retain.                     1920

Cast down thyself, and only strive to raise
The glory of thy Maker's sacred Name;
Use all thy powers, that Blessed Power to praise,
Which gives the power to *be*, and *use the same*.          1924

**FINIS.**

# Metaphrase of Some Psalms[1]

### Psalm I.

That man is blest which hath not walked aside,
Taking ungodly counsel for his guide;
Nor in the way of sinners stood and stayed,
Nor in the couch of Scorners down him laid,
But in God's Law hath placed his whole delight,
And studieth to perform it, day and night:
He, like a plant which by a stream doth grow,
His timely fruit shall in due season show;
Whose leaf shall not decay but flourish ever,
And all things prosper which he doth endeavor
But with th' ungodly it shall not be so,
But as the dust, which as the whirlwinds to and fro
Upon the surface of the earth doth drive,
They shall a restless life and fruitless live;
Nor shall they stand upright when they are tried,
Nor in the assembly of the just abide:
But in his way God doth the good man cherish,
When wicked men in their bad way shall perish.

### Psalm II.

Why do the nations thus in fury rise?
Why do the people such vain plots devise?
Monarchs stand up and Princes do conspire
Against the Lord, and His Anointed Heir:
'Let us in sunder break their bands,' say they,
'And let us lightly cast their yokes away.'
But He that sits in Heaven shall them deride,
And laugh to scorn their folly and their pride;
And in His wrath He shall reprove them sore,
And vex them in His anger, more and more:
Saying, 'I set on Sion hill My King,

---

1  Unpublished in Davies' lifetime

To preach my Law, and show this heavenly thing;
Thou art My Son, this day I Thee begot,
Ask, and I will assign thee for Thy Lot
Of heritage the Lands and Nations all,
Between the Sun's uprising & his fall.'
Thou with an iron rod shall keep them under,
And break them like an earthen pot in sunder,
Be wise, ye Monarchs, and ye Princes then;
Be learnèd, ye that judge the sons of men;
Serve ye the Lord, with humble fear Him serve;
Rejoice in Him, yet trembling Him observe;
Kiss ye the Son, lest ye Him angry make,
And perish, while His just ways ye forsake,
If His just wrath but once inclined be:
Who trust in Him, a blessed man is he.

### Psalm III.

ord! how my foes in number do increase,
That rise against me, to disturb my peace!
MANY there are which to my soul have said,
His God to him not safety yields nor aid;
But God is my defense, my Succor nigh,
My glory, and my head He lifteth High:
To Him with earnest prayer appealèd I,
And from His Holy Hill He heard my cry:
I laid me down and slept, and rose again,
For me the Lord doth evermore sustain:
Though Thousand of my foes beset me round,
No fear of them my courage shall confound:
Rise Lord! and save me; Thou hast given a stroke
On my foes' cheek, that all his teeth are broke:
Salvation cometh from this Lord of ours,
Who blessings on His people daily pours.

### Psalm IV.

God! whose righteousness by grace is mine,
A gracious ear unto my voice incline:
Thou that hast set me free when I was thrall,
Be merciful, and hear my prayer withal.
Vain, worldly men, how long will ye despise
God's honor, and His truth, and trust in lies?
God for Himself, the good man doth select,
And when I cry He doth not me reject.
Be angry, but be angry without sin;
Try your own hearts in silence, close within.
To God, of godly works, an offering make,
Then trust in Him that will not His forsake.
For that which good is, many seek and pray,
'And who shall show the same to us'? say they,
Lord! show to us thy countenance divine,
And cause the Beams thereof on us to shine:
So shall my heart more joyful be and glad,
Then if increase of corn and wine I had.
To peace therefore lie down will I and sleep
For God alone doth me in safety keep.

### Psalm V.

ORD weigh my words, and take consideration
Of my sad thoughts and silent meditation:
My God, my King, bow down Thine ear to me,
While I send up mine humble prayer to Thee.
Early, before the morn doth bring the day,
I will O Lord, look up to Thee and pray:
For Thou with sin art never pleasèd well,
Nor any ill may with Thy goodness dwell:
The fool may not before Thy wisdom stand,
Nor shall the impious scape Thy wrathful hand:
Thou wilt destroy all such as utter lies;
Blood and deceit are odious in Thine eyes;
But, trusting in Thy many mercies dear,
I will approach Thy house with holy fear.

Teach me Thy plain and righteous way to go,
That I may never fall before my foe,
Whose flattering tongue is false and heart impure,
And throat, an open place of Sepulture.
Destroy them, Lord, and frustrate their devices,
Cast out those Rebels for their many vices;
But all that trust in Thee and love Thy name,
Make them rejoice and rescue them from shame.
Thou wilt thy blessing to the righteous yield
And guard them with Thy grace as with a Shield.

## Psalm VI.

 o judge me, Lord, in Thy just wrath forbear,
To punish me in thy displeasure spare;
O! I am weak: have mercy, Lord, therefore,
And heal my bruisèd bones which pain me sore.
My Soul is also troubled and dismayed;
But, Lord, how long shall I expect Thine aid!
Turn Thee, O Lord, my Soul from death deliver,
Even for Thy mercy's sake which lasteth ever:
They which are dead remember not Thy name,
Nor doth the silent Grave thy praise proclaim;
I faint and melt away with griefs and fears,
And every night my bed doth swim with tears.
Mine eyes are sunk and weakened is my sight;
My foes have vexèd me with such despite.
Away from me, ye sinful men, away!
The LORD of Heaven doth hear me when I pray.
The Lord hath my petition heard indeed:
Receive my prayer and I shall surely speed;
But shame and sorrow on my foes shall light,
They shall be turn'd and put to sudden flight.

### Psalm VII.

 Lord, my God! I put my trust in Thee,
From all my Persecutors rescue me:
Lest my proud foe doth like a lion rend me,
While there is none to succour and defend me:
Lord God! if I be guilty found in this,
Wherewith my foes have chargèd me amiss,
If I did use my friend unfriendly so,
Nay, if I did not help my causeless foe,
Let him prevail, although my cause be just,
And lay my life and honor in the dust.
Up, Lord! and stand against my furious foes,
Thy Judgment against them for me disclose;
So shall Thy People flock about Thee nigh,
For their sakes therefore lift Thyself on high.
Judge of the world, give sentence on my part,
According to the cleanness of my heart:
Let wickedness be brought unto an end,
And guide the just, that they may not offend.
Thou God art just, and Thou the Searcher art
Of heart and reins[2] and every inward part:
My help proceedeth from the Lord of Might,
Who saveth those which are of heart upright;
A powerful and a patient Judge is He,
Though every day His wrath provokèd be:
But, if men will not turn, His sword He whets,
And bends His bow, and to the string He sets
The Instruments of death, His arrows keen,
'Gainst such as rebels to His will have been.
The impious man conceives iniquity,
Travails with mischief, and brings forth a lie:
The Righteous to entrap he digs a pit,
But he himself first falls and sinks in it.
The wicked plots his working brain doth cast,
Light with a mischief on himself at last.
*My thanks with God's great justice shall accord,*
and I will highly praise the highest Lord.

---

2  The kidneys

## Psalm VIII.

God, our Lord! How great is the extent
Of Thy great name and glory excellent!
It fills this world, but it doth shine most bright
Above the heavens, in th' unapproachèd light.
By sucking babes thy strength dost Thou disclose,
And by their mouth to silence put Thy foes.
When I see Heaven wrought by Thy mighty hand,
And all those glorious lights in order stand,
Lord! what is man that Thou on him dost look!
Or of the Son of Man such care hast took!
Next Angels in degree Thou hast him placed,
And with a crown of honor hast him graced:
Thou hast him made lord of Thy Creatures all,
Subjecting them to his command and call;
All birds and airy fowls are under him,
And fishes all which in the Sea do swim.
O Lord, our God! how large is the extent
Of Thy great name and glory excellent!

## Psalm IX.

hee will I thank ever with my heart entire,
And make the world Thy wondrous works admire;
In Thee rejoice, in Thee triumph will I,
My songs shall praise Thy name, O God, most High!
While my proud foes are put to shameful flight,
And fall and perish at Thy dreadful sight.
Thou, righteous Judge, dost sit upon Thy Throne
And dost maintain my rightful cause alone;
Thou check the Heathen; and the wicked race
Thou dost destroy, and all their names deface.
O Enemy! behold thy final fall,
Thy Cities perish and their names withal;
But God, our Lord, for ever shall endure,
His judgement Seat, He hath established sure,
Where He judges the World with equal right,
And measures Justice unto every weight:

He likewise will become a Bulwark strong
And timely aid to them that suffer wrong.
Who knows Thy name in Thee his trust will place,
Who never failest them that seek Thy face.
O, praise the Lord! you that in Sion dwell,
His noble Acts among the Nations tell;
When of oppression He enquiry makes,
Of every poor man's plaint He notice takes.
Have mercy, Lord! and take into Thy thought
My troubles, which my hateful foes have wrought.
Thou from the gates of death my Soul dost raise,
That I in Sion's Gates may sing Thy praise;
The sweet salvation which Thou dost impart
Shall be the joy and comfort of my heart.
The Infidels make pits, and sink therein,
Their feet are caught in their own proper sin;
Thy judgement Lord, Thou hast thereby declared
When wicked men in their own works are snared:
Hell is a place for impious men assign'd
And such as do cast God out of their mind;
But poor men shall not be forgotten ever
Nor meek mens' patience, if they do persevere.
Rise Lord! and let not man above Thee rise
And judge the Infidel with angry eyes:
Strike them with fear, that, though they know not Thee,
Yet they may know that mortal men they be.

## Psalm X.

hy standest Thou O Lord! so far away
And hide Thy face when troubles me dismay?
The wicked for his lust the poor man spoils;
Lord! take him in the trap of his own wiles.
He makes his boast of his profane desires
Condemning God, while he himself admires:
He is so proud, that God he sets at nought,
Nay rather, God comes never in his thought.
Thy judgements Lord, are far above his sight

This makes him to esteem his foes so light,
And in his heart to say, I cannot fall,
Nor can misfortune light on me at all:
His mouth is full of execrations vile;
Under his tongue doth sit ungodly guile;
Close in the corners of the ways he lies,
And lurks, and waits, the simple to surprise:
Even as a lion lurking in his den,
To assault and murder innocent poor men;
'Gainst whom his eyes maliciously are set,
To catch them when they fall into his net.
Himself he humbles, bows, and crouching stands
Till poor men fall into his powerful hands;
Then, in his heart he saith 'God hath forgot:
He turns away his face and sees it not.'
Arise O Lord! and lift Thy hand on high,
The poor forget not which oppressèd lie:
For why should wicked men blaspheme Thee thus
'Tush! God is careless and regards not us'?
Surely Thou sees the wrong which they have done,
And all oppressions underneath the sun;
To Thee alone the poor his cause commends
As th' only friend of him that wanteth friends.
Lord! break the power of the malicious mind
Take ill away, and Thou not ill shalt find.
The Lord is king, and doth for ever reign,
Nor miscreants shall within His Land remain;
He hearkeneth to the poor, but first prepareth
Their hearts to pray; then their petition heareth:
That He poor orphans, may both help and save,
That worldly men on them no power may have.

## Psalm XI.

trust in God: to me why should you say,
'Fly like a bird to mountains far away'?
Their bows and arrows wicked men prepare,
To pierce the hearts of them that faithful are:
Even him whom God hath made a corner-stone
They have cast down; but what hath He misdone?
God in His holy temple doth remain,
The heaven of Heavens: where He doth sit and reign.
Upon the poor He casteth down His eye,
The sons of Men He doth discern and try;
The just and righteous men He doth approve,
But hateth sinners which their sins do love;
On them He raineth snares, brimstone and fire,
This is their cup, their wages, and their hire;
The righteous God loves him whose way is right,
And on the just His gracious eye doth light.

## Psalm XII.

elp Lord! for all the godly men are gone,
And of the faithful, few there are, or none;
Each man to other doth vain things impart,
With lips deceitful, and with double heart;
The Lord will soon cut off the lips that lie,
And root out tongues that speak proud words and high.
'With mighty words we will prevail' say they:
What Lord is He that dareth us gainsay?'
'Now for the troubles and oppressions sore
The groanings and the sighings of the poor,
I will arise' saith God, 'and quell their foes
That swell with pride; and them in rest repose.'
God's words are pure, and chaste, like silver tried
Which hath with seven fires been purified.
Thou wilt preserve them Lord! and guard them still,
From this vile race of men which wish them ill.
The ungodly walk in circles, yet go free
When such as fear not God, exalted be.

## Psalm XIII.

ow long O Lord! shall I forgotten be?
How long wilt Thou Thy bright Face hide from me?
How long shall I my thoughts toss to and fro
And be thus vexed by my insulting foe?
Give ease, O Lord; give light unto mine eyes,
Lest death in endless sleep doth me surprise;
Lest my proud foe vaunt that he doth prevail,
And laugh at me when I shall faint or fail;
But in Thy mercy all my trust is pight[3]
And thy salvation is my heart's delight;
Of Thy sweet kindness therefore sing will I,
And highly praise the name of God, Most High.

## Psalm XIV.

here is no God,' The Fool saith in his heart,
Yet dares not with his tongue his thought impart;
All are corrupt and odious in God's sight,
Not one doth good, not one doth well, upright.
God cast His eyes from Heaven on all mankind,
And looked if He one righteous man could find;
But all were wicked, all from God were gone,
Not one did good, in all the world, not one;
Their throat an open grave, their flattering tongue
And lying lips, like sting of wasps have stung.
With bitter cursing, they their mouths do fill;
Their feet are swift the guiltless blood to spill;
Sad, wretched mischief, in their ways doth lie
But for the ways of peace they pass them by;
No fear of God have they before their eyes,
Nor knowledge, while these mischiefs they devise;
While they God's people do with might oppress
And eat them up like bread with greediness;
And since on God they never use to call,
They fear'd when cause of fear was none at all.

---

3   Pitched

But to the righteous man and to his race,
God present is with His protecting grace;
Though fools do mock the counsel of the poor,
Because in God he trusted evermore.
Who shall salvation out of Sion give
To Israel but God? Who shall relieve
His people and of captives make them free:
Thou Jacob joyful, Israel glad shall be.

## Psalm XV.

ord! Who shall dwell in Thy bright tent with Thee
And of Thy rest in heaven partaker be?
Even he that is upright in all his ways
And from his heart speaks truth in all he says;
Who hath forborne to do his neighbor wrong
Nor him deceived or slanderèd with his tongue;
Who of himself a humble thought doth bear
But highly values them which God do fear;
Who of his promise doth himself acquit,
Though loss he suffer by performing it;
Nor hath for biting use his money lent,
Nor took reward against the innocent;
Who shall observe these points, and do them all,
Assuredly that man can never fall.

## Psalm XVI.

e thy poor servant Lord! preserve and save,
For all my trust in Thee repos'd I have:
Lord! said my soul, Thou art my God, to Thee
My goods are nothing when they offered be;
But my delights are in those saints of Thine,
Which live on Earth, and do in virtue shine;
But they which run to worship idols vain,
Shall multiply their sorrow and their pain.
Of their blood offerings will I not partake,
Nor of their names shall my lips mention make.

The portion of mine heritage and cup
Is God Himself who holds and keeps me up;
In a faire ground to me my lot did chance,
So I possess a rich Inheritance:
Thanks be to God His warning gives me light,
My reins with pain do chasten me by night;
I look to God in my endeavors all,
He stands so near me that I cannot fall;
This hath my heart and tongue with joys possessed,
And now my flesh in hope to rise, shall rest;
My soul shall not be buried in the grave,
Nor shall Thy Holy One corruption have;
Show me the path of life; for in Thy sight
Doth endless pleasure rest and full delight.

### Psalm XVII.

 ear my just cause Lord! hear my prayer and cry,
Which come from lips not us'd to fain or lie:
Lord, let my sentence from Thy mouth be given,
For Thou regards't things only just and even;
In the dark night of my adversity,
Thou did'st my heart examine, prove and try;
And yet upon this trial did not find
My heart or tongue to any ill inclined:
For that their works against Thy Word are done
I do their ways which tend to ruin, shun.
Lord! in Thy paths do Thou my goings guide,
Lest in this slippery life my footsteps slide:
Thy name have I invoked, Thou shalt me hear
And to my humble words incline Thy ear;
O Saviour! of all those that trust in Thee
Thy mercies full of wonder show to me;
Preserve me as the apple of Thine eye,
Under Thy wings in safety let me lie;
Save me from them which Thy right hand oppose,
And from my ungodly circumventing foes;
Their fat estates do them so fortify
As they presume to speak proud words and high;

In all my ways in wait for me he lies,
To cast me down he downwards casts his eyes
Even like a lion, watching for his prey,
Or lion's whelps which lurk beside the way.
Up Lord! defeat, defeat this foe of mine,
That wicked man who is a sword of Thine;
From worldly men vouchsafe my soul to save,
Who in their mortal life their portion have;
Whose bellies with Thy treasure Thou dost fill,
Who children have, and leave them wealth at will;
But I Thy face in righteousness shall see
And with Thy presence shall contented be.

## Psalm XVIII.

hou art my strength, O Lord! Thee will I love,
Thou art my Rock, which nothing can remove:
My God, in Whom my trust I will repose,
My Savior, shield and horn, against my foes;
Lord, most praiseworthy, pray will I to Thee
So shall I from my foes protected be;
When deadly sorrows did beset me round,
And floods of wickedness did me surround
When pains of hell I felt in my disease,
And pangs of death upon my soul did cease;
On God I callèd in that instant trouble,
And my complaints unto the Lord did double:
But when His wrath and vengeance kindled were,
The Earth did quake, and mountains shook for fear,
And coals grew red with His inflaming ire;
He bowed the heavens, and did descend withal,
And shadows dark beneath His feet did fall:
He riding on the Cherubims did fly,
And with the wingèd winds was borne on high;
Darkness His closet, His pavilion wide
Made of black clouds, His face a while did hide;
But at His presence right away they flew
When hail and coals of fire abroad He threw;
The Lord from heaven did send His thunder loud

With fire and hail from out the broken cloud;
A shower of arrows on His foes did fall,
His thunderbolts and lightenings slew them all;
Fountains were dried and the earth's foundation moved
When sinners, in His wrath, the Lord reproved;
But He from heaven shall send His angels down
And take me up when waters would me drown;
He from my foe, too mightie and too strong,
Shall save me when He doth me mightie wrong,
Preventing me in my disastrous day:
But then the Lord was my support and stay;
When I was captive, He did set me free,
And brought me forth because He favored me.
He shall reward me as my days be right,
And hands be clean: so shall He me requite;
For I still kept his paths, and did not shun
To walk therein, as other men have done:
But ever set His laws before mine eyes,
And never did His holy words despise.
My heart was uncorrupt before Him still,
Pursuing goodness and eschewing ill;
He shall reward me as my deeds be right,
And hands be clean: so shall He me requite.
Unto the good Thou wilt Thy goodness show,
And righteous men Thy righteousness shall know;
The pure of heart shall Thee behold most pure
But froward men Thy curses shall endure;
Them will God raise, which under pressures lie,
And proud men humble which do look so high;
He shall set up for me a candle bright,
My God shall turn my darkness unto light.
Through Thee, a host of men, I conquer shall,
And with Thy help transcend the highest wall;
God's way is pure, His word is tried with fire;
He heals all them which unto Him retire;
For who is God? or who hath strength and power
Except our Lord, our God and only our?
He girdeth me with furniture to fight,
And guideth me, and holdeth me upright;

My feet as swift as Hart's feet He doth make,
And up to honor's tower He doth me take;
He gives such strength unto my fingers weak,
As that my arm a bow of steel shall break.
Thy hands shall be my safety and protection,
Thou shalt advance me with Thy sweet correction;
Thou for my feet shalt make a passage wide,
So as my steps shall never go aside;
I shall pursue, and in pursuit outgo,
And never turn till I have quelled my foe;
When I him smite he shall not rise at all,
If once at my victorious feet he fall.
Thou hast girded me with a sword of strength,
Wherewith I shall subdue my foes at length;
For thou shalt turn the stubborn neck about
Of them that hate me till I root them out;
Then shall they cry (but help there shall be none)
Even to the Lord, Who shall not hear their moan.
My foes to powder I shall break and bray[4]
And tread them down like mire amid the way.
Thou my rebellious subjects shalt accord,
And over Heathen Nations make me Lord;
A people whom I know not shall me serve,
And with base adulation me observe;
These Aliens all shall faint and be dismayed
And in their strongest Castles be afraid.
Live Lord! my strength: and blessed be therefore
And praisèd be my Savior evermore,
Who doth repay my foes with vengeance due,
And unto me my vassals doth subdue;
Who doth not only save but set me high
Above my foes, and their fierce cruelty.
For this, both of my thanks and praise to Thee,
The Heathen Nations witnesses shall be;
For wealth and power and blessings many mo,
On David and his race Thou shalt bestow.

---

4  To crush or grind fine

## Psalm XIX.

he workmanship of heaven so bright and fair,
Thy power O Lord, and glory doth declare;
One day Thy praise doth to another preach,
One night another doth in order teach;
Where ever any tongue or voice doth sound,
In all the world their speech is heard around.
In midst of heav'n, the hands of God hath pight
For the sun's lodging, a pavilion bright;
Who as a bridegroom from his chamber goes;
Or Giant, marching forth against his foes,
He issues; and from East to West doth run:
His piercing heat no living weight can shun.
God's law is perfect and man's soul renews,
And simple minds with knowledge it endues;
Right are His statutes and rejoice the heart,
Light to the eyes His precepts pure impart;
His fear is clean and so endures for aye;
His judgements true and righteous every way;
More sweet then honey, to be valued more
Then many heaps of finest golden ore.
They rectify withal Thy servant's mind,
And who so keeps them, great reward shall find;
But Lord who knows how oft he doth transgress?
O cleanse me from my secret wickedness!
Nor let presumptuous sins bear rule in me,
So shall I from the great offense be free;
And Lord! my strength and Savior! so direct
My words and thoughts as Thou mayest them accept.

## Psalm XX.

he Lord give ear to thee in thy distress!
And be thy Shield, when troubles thee oppress!
And let His help come down from heaven for thee!
And strength from Sion Hill imparted be!
Let Him remember, and accept withal,
Thine offerings and thy sacrifices all;

And of His bounty evermore fulfill
Thy heart's desire; and satisfy thy will.
But we will glory in our great God's name
And joy in our salvation through the same;
And pray unto the Lord our God, that He
The effect of all thy prayers will grant to thee.
He now I know will hear, and help will bring,
With His strong hand to His anointed King;
On chariots some, on horses some, rely,
But we invoke the name of God Most High.
Those others are bowed down and fall full low,
When we are risen and upright do go.
Save us O Lord of Heaven! and hear us thence,
When we invoke Thy name for our defense.

## Psalm XXI.

lad is the king, and joyful is his heart,
That Thou O Lord, his strength and safety art;
That Thou hast given him what his heart desired,
And not denied him what his lips required;
Preventing him with blessings manifold,
And crowning him with pure refinèd gold.
He asked Thee life, Thou gavest him length of days,
Even endless life, to give Thee endless praise;
His safety, through Thy providence divine
With honor great and glory makes him shine;
Bliss without end Thou wilt to him impart,
The sun-beams of Thy face will cheer his heart:
For in Thy mercy he doth trust withal,
Which stays his steps that he shall never fall;
But Thy long hand shall reach Thy flying foe
And find him when he most secure doth go;
Thine enemies shall (when kindled is Thine ire)
As in a furnace be consumed with fire;
Their offspring from the Earth shall rotted be,
Their second generation none shall see:
For against Thee and Thine their counsel was,
Yet could not bring their wicked plot to pass,

But turn'd their backs and put themselves to chase,
When Thou hadst bent Thy bow against their face;
Be pleased in Thine own strength Thyself to raise,
So shall we, Lord, Thy power and mercy praise.

## Psalm XXII.

y God! my God! why leavest Thou me? and why
Dost Thou so far withdraw Thee from my cry?
I cry all day, but Thou dost not give ear;
At night I cease not, yet Thou wilt not hear;
Yet Thou art holy still, Thou God of might,
Thy people's great renown and glory bright;
When our forefathers placed their hope in Thee
From cruel bondage Thou didst set them free;
In Thee they trusted, and to Thee they prayed,
And never failed of Thy celestial aid;
But as for me, a worm not man, am I;
A scorn to every man that passeth by;
They laugh and mock, my poor estate to see;
They draw their mouth and shake their heads at me;
And say, 'He hop't in God, that He should save him,
Now let God rescue him if He will have him.'
But Thou Lord from my mother's womb didst take me,
And when I sucked her breast, didst not forsake me;
Even from my birth I was to Thee bequeathèd,
And Thou hast been my God since first I breathèd.
O leave me not when troubles do me press,
And there is none to help me in distress;
Many strong beasts have me environèd
As fat and fierce as bulls in Bashan fed;
They run on me with open mouths and wide;
Like hungry lions ramping in their pride.
My soul, like water on the earth is spilt,
My joints are loosed, my heart like wax doth melt,
My sinews shrunk are, like a potsherd dry,
My tongue cleaves to my jaws, dead dust am I.
For many dogs have compassed me about,
I am beset with a malicious rout;

They pierce My hands and feet, and stare on Me,
And every rib of My lean body see;
They spoil Me of My Garments, and beside,
The parts thereof by lots they do divide.
Lord! be not far, when I Thy help shall need,
Thou art My strength, O succour Me with speed!
And shield Me from the sword, and from the power
Of dogs, which would My dearest Soul devour!
And from the lion's mouth, and from the horns
Of many, fierce, insulting unicorns!
Among My kin will I declare Thy name,
And in the great Assembly spread the same.
Ye that fear Him His praise and glory tell,
And honor Him ye seed of Israel;
He scorneth not the poor, nor hides His face,
But hears his suit when he laments his case.
When all Thy faithful folk assembled be,
I sound Thy praise and pay my vows to Thee.
The Lord shall fully satisfy the meek,
Their soul shall live which His light face do seek;
The East and West shall turn to their right mind,
And to the true God's worship be inclined;
Who doth, of all the world the Scepter bear,
Rules and commands the nations everywhere;
The fat shall eat and worship Him therefore,
And they that lie in dust shall Him adore.
Even he which cannot his own life preserve,
Nor quicken his own soul, the Lord shall serve.
Their seed, O Lord! shall serve to worship Thee,
And with Thy chosen people numbered be;
And to their children's children, shall express
Thine everlasting truth and righteousness.

## Psalm XXIII.

he Lord my Shepherd is, He doth me feed,
His bounty evermore supplies my need;
When I in pastures green my fill have took,
He leads me forth into the silver brook;
He turns my soul, when it is gone astray,
For His name's glory, to His righteous way;
Therefore although my soul detruded[5] were,
Even to Hell's gates, yet I not ill should fear;
When Thou art with me, what should me dismay?
Thy crook, my comfort is; Thy staff, my stay;
My table Thou hast spread and furnished so,
As glads my heart, and grieves my envious foe;
Thy balm pour'd on my head, doth sweetly smell;
Thou makes my cup above the brim to swell.
Thy mercy, while I breathe, shall follow me,
And in Thy house my dwelling-place shall be.

## Psalm XXIV.

he Earth, and all things which on the Earth remain,
Even all the world, doth to the Lord pertain;
Amid the Sea, He founded hath the Land
And made this Globe above the floods to stand.
Who shall unto Jehovah's Mount ascend?
Or who shall in His holy place attend?
Even he whose hands are clean, whose heart is pure,
Whose tongue is true, whose oath is just and sure.
He shall receive both righteousness and bliss
From God, Whose mercy his salvation is.
Such are the seed of Jacob's faithful race,
Which seek the Lord, and love to see His face;
Ye everlasting Gates, your heads uprear,
And let the King of Glory enter there.
That glorious name, to Whom doth it belong?
To God Most Mightie and in war most strong.

5   Thrust down

Eternal doors, lift up your heads, I say
That there, the King of Glory enter may.
The King of Glory enters, what is He?
The Lord of Hosts is known that King to ee.

## Psalm XXV.

ine humble soul O Lord! I lift to Thee,
On Whom my trust shall ever fixèd be;
O suffer not my cheeks with shame to glow,
Nor make me slave to my insulting foe;
For they which hope in Thee incur no blame,
But willful sinners shall be clothed with shame.
To me, O Lord! vouchsafe Thy ways to show,
And Thy right paths, that I therein may go;
Teach me the way of truth, direct my will;
Thou art my Savior, I attend Thee still;
Receive me Lord, and to remembrance call
Thy old compassions, and Thy mercies all;
But of Thy wonted grace to me, O Lord
Of the errors of my youth keep no record;
The Lord is good, and for His goodness' sake
He teaches sinners, godly ways to take;
Yet He His learning doth to none impart
But to the meek and to the humble heart;
His paths are grace and truth; that only way
He leads all those which do His will obey.
For Thy name's glory, I do Thee entreat
To my great sins, extend Thy mercy great
To him which fears the Lord, the Lord doth show
How in his calling he may safely go;
His soul shall be at ease and all his race,
Shall in the Land possess a blessed place;
His covenant and His counsels near,
God shows to them in whom He plants His fear;
My look to Him shall ever raisèd be,
Who from the net my captive feet doth free.
Have mercy Lord on me! and turn Thy face
To see my desolate and wither'd case;

Enlargèd is my grief and heaviness,
But Lord, enlarge Thou me from my distress!
Look on the woful State that I am in;
Remit the cause thereof, which is my sin;
My foes consider, and their multitude
Which me with deadly hatred hath pursued;
And keep my soul from sin, my face from shame,
Who trust in Thee and call upon Thy name.
Let truth and righteousness without deceit
Still wait on me, because on Thee I wait;
And set Thy faithful Israel at rest
From all the troubles which do him molest.

## Psalm XXVI.

 e thou my Judge, O LORD! my cause is just;
I shall not stagger while in Thee I trust.
Weigh and examine me, search all my veins,
The bottom of my heart and inward reins;
I set Thy goodness ever in my sight,
Which in Thy truth doth guide my steps aright;
I use not to converse with persons vain,
Nor with dissemblers fellowship retain;
My soul the assembly of the wicked hates.
Nor will I sit among ungodly Mates;
Repentance having made my conscience clear,
Then will I Lord, approach Thine Altar near;
That I may thank Thee both with heart and voice,
And telling of Thy wondrous works rejoice
Thy temple Lord, I love exceeding well,
Wherein Thy Majesty and Glory dwell.
O let not sinful men my soul enclose,
Nor of my life let sinful men dispose;
Whose hands are foul, their sins them foul do make,
And full of gifts which they corruptly take;
But I to leave a blameless life intend:
O Lord therein with mercy me defend.
My foot stands right and therefore all my days
In all assemblies I the Lord will praise.

## Psalm XXVII.

od is my Light, Salvation, strength, and aid,
Of whom and what shall I then be afraid?
The wicked came to have devour'd me quite,
But stumbled in their way, and fell down-right.
Though mighty armies in my ways were laid,
I stand secure, I cannot be dismayed.
One thing I wish, even while I live to dwell,
In God's faire House, where beauty doth excel;
His tent, in time of trouble, shall me hide,
And I shall on His rock of safety bide;
Now shall He lift my head above my foes,
Which me with armèd multitudes, enclose;
And now will I His praise in triumph sing,
And joyful offerings to His temple bring;
And let my cries approach Thy gracious ear,
Vouchsafe in mercy my complaints to hear;
My heart doth tell that Thou bid'st me still
Thy face to seek: Lord! seek Thy face I will.
Then do not hide from me Thy face so bright,
Nor in Thy wrath exclude me from Thy sight;
Thou ever wast mine aid, since I was borne:
God of my safety, leave me not forlorn.
My father and my mother both forsook me,
But then the Lord to his tuition[6] took me;
Teach me the way that I therein may go,
So shall I never fall before my foe;
Nor fall into their power which do me hate,
And brought false oaths against me in the gate.
My heart had fail'd but that my hope to see
God's endless bliss in heaven did comfort me.
Then stay God's time, He shall thee stay at length,
And He till then shall arm thy heart with strength.

---

6  Instruction

## Psalm XXVIII.

ear (Lord my strength!) the cry I make to Thee!
I am but dead, if Thou seem deaf to me:
Hear, when with humble prayer, I Thee entreat,
With lifted hands before Thy mercy seat.
But rank me not with those which wicked are,
Whose lips speak peace, whose hearts are full of war;
According to their actions let them speed,
And as their merit is, so make their need;
For that they see Thy works, and yet neglect them,
Thou shall destroy and never more erect them:
The Lord be praised Who hath vouchsafed to hear,
And lend unto my prayer a gracious ear;
His Shield protects, His strength doth me advance;
My tongue shall sing His praise, my heart shall dance;
He to His servants, force, and virtue, gives;
Through Him in safety His anointed lives.
Save Thy peculiar people, Lord! and bless them,
And lift their heads above them that oppress them.

## Psalm XXIX.

e kings, since by God's power and grace, ye reign,
Glory and power ascribe to Him again;
Yield Him the honor due to His great name,
And in His glorious Courts, His praise proclaim;
His voice doth cause the Seas to swell and shake,
And in the heavens the dreadful thunder make;
Jehovah's voice, effects of power doth breed,
It is a strong and glorious voice indeed;
His voice the cedar doth in sunder tear,
The Cedars which Mount Lebanus doth bear;
Makes Lebanus, and Hermon hill, to tremble
And skipping Calves and Unicorns, resemble;
Doth break the clouds, and flames of fire divide,
The deserts shake, even Cades[7] desert wide;

---

7  Kadesh

Makes hinds to calve, for fear makes forests bare,
While in His temple we His praise declare;
The Lord upon the water-floods doth reign,
The Lord a King for ever doth remain;
The Lord shall still His people's strength increase,
And give to them the blessing of His peace.

## Psalm XXX.

ighly the Lord I praise Who sets me high
Above my proud insulting enemy;
Sick to the death, I cried to God for ease,
And He hath cur'd my dangerous disease;
He from the grave hath lifted up my head
And hath reduced me from among the dead.
Ye Saints of His in songs His praise express,
With thanks make mention of His holiness;
For momentary His displeasure is,
When in His favor there is life and bliss;
Sad sorrow may continue for a night,
But joy returneth with the morning light.
When my estate did prosper, then said I
I shall not fall, my seat is fixed on high.
But when Thou Lord, didst turn Thy face aside,
Then was I troubled, and to Thee I cried;
To Thee began I then again to pray,
And in my humble prayer thus did say:
What profit can there by my death arise,
When buried in the grave my body lies?
Shall dust and ashes celebrate Thy name?
Or shall the silent Tomb Thy truth proclaim?
Lord, hear my prayer, and then Thy mercy show
In aiding me against my cruel foe!
Lo now to dancing, Thou hast turn'd my sadness,
Out of my sackcloth girded me with gladness.
For this shall every good man sing Thy praise,
And I shall thank and bless Thee all my days.

## *Psalm XXXI.*

n Thee, O Lord! have I put all my trust,
Then rescue me from shame, as Thou art just;
Give ear, and soon from peril set me free;
Be Thou a Rock and strong defense to me;
Thou art my Rock and Castle when I stray;
Be Thou my Guide, and lead me in the way.
Thou art my strength; O clear me from that net
Which privily my foes for me have set!
Into Thy hands my soul I do commit:
LORD God of truth Thou hast redeemèd it.
I hate all those which in vain lies delight,
For all my trust is in the Lord of might.
Thy mercies glad my heart: for in my woe
Thou hast vouchsafed my weary soul to know.
Thou hast not left me prisoner with my foe,
But set me free that I at large may go.
Yield to my troubles merciful relief,
My ears wax deaf, my heart doth melt with grief.
Few are my years, in number to be told,
Yet sorrow, care, and grief, hath made me old;
My strength with prayer and anguish doth decay,
My joints grow weak, my bones consume away;
I am a scorn to all my enemies,
But specially my Neighbors me despise;
My very presence did my friends affright,
And all my old acquaintance shun my sight.
I am forgot as if I buried lay,
And viler than a broken pot of clay.
I heard the wailings of the multitude
And trembled while they did my death conclude;
But all my hope hath been O Lord in Thee,
Whom I profess my only Lord to be;
My time is in Thy hand, O do not leave
Me in their hands which would my life bereave.
O turn to me the brightness of Thy face,
And save me through Thy mercy and Thy grace;
Make not me blush which did invoke Thy name,

But put my foes to silence and to shame;
And let the lips be dumb which utter lies
Against the righteous in spiteful-wise.
O what blessings, dost Thou keep in store
For them that fear and love Thee evermore;
Thou shalt protect them from the great men's pride,
And in Thy Tent from storms of tongues them hide.
Blest be the Lord Whose mercies manifold
Do keep me safer than the strongest hold;
When I with passion was transported quite,
I said I was sequester'd from His sight;
And yet for all my weakness, heard was I,
When to my Maker I did make my cry.
Love Him ye Saints of His who guardeth those
Who trust in Him: and pays their proudest foes.
Ye that rely on Him be strong of heart
And He to you shall heavenly strength impart.

## Psalm XXXII.

 appy indeed and truly blest is he
Whose sins remitted and faults coverèd be;
To whom the Lord doth not impute his sin,
Whose single heart hath not deceit therein.
When I was silent I consumed away,
And pining grief did waste me day by day;
Thy hand on me was heavy still, whereby
My moisture grew like draught in Summer dry.
My sin I will acknowledge Lord to Thee,
My secret faults shall not concealèd be;
I said, I will my sins to God confess,
And God forthwith forgave my wickedness.
If good men seek Him when He may be found,
The world's high waves shall never them surround;
Thou hid'st me close and savest me from annoy,
And dost environ me with songs of joy;
When Thou hast set me in Thine own right way,
Thine eye doth guide me that I do not stray.
Then must I not be brute, as horse and mule,

Which men with bit and bridle only rule.
With many whips, God doth the wicked chase
But doth with mercies faithful men embrace;
Be glad, rejoice, and glory in the Lord
All ye whose hearts doth with His will accord.

## Psalm XXXIII.

 ejoice ye righteous in the Lord, and sing;
To give God thanks, it is a comely thing:
Sing praises unto Him and set your songs
To harp and lute, that speaketh with ten tongues;
Sing to the Lord a new composèd song,
With cheerful heart and with affection strong;
For His most holy Word is ever true,
And all His works His constancy do shew.
He loveth right and justice evermore,
And with His blessing He the earth doth store;
For by His word the heavens created were;
His breath made every Star and every sphere;
The Seas, as in a Storehouse He doth keep,
And heaps them up as treasures in the deep;
The earth before the LORD shall quake for fear,
And all that dwell on His round Center here:
He spake, and they were made; at His command
The heavens began to move, the earth to stand.
Counsels of princes and of Nations great,
And peoples' plots, His wisdom doth defeat;
But God's own counsel, purpose and decree,
Eternal stand, and cannot frustrate be.
That Nation hath true happiness and bliss,
Whose God and LORD, the LORD Jehovah is;
Down from the highest heaven the Lord did look,
And of all men a full survey He took;
From Heaven above the Lord did cast His eye,
And all men's ways and wanderings did espy.
He formèd all their hearts, and understands
Their thoughts, their words, and works of all their hands.
The greatest armies cannot save a King,

Nor strength unto a strong man safety bring;
His trust is vain who trusteth in his horse,
And seeks deliverance by so small a force;
With gracious eye the Lord beholds the just,
Which Him do fear and in His mercy trust:
In time of dearth their hungry souls to feed
And from death's jaws to rescue them with speed.
Our souls with patience for the Lord have staid,
Who is our only shield, support, and aid;
Our hearts shall Him as our true joy embrace,
For we our only trust in Him do place.
Thy mercy Lord to us exceeded be,
According to the hope we have in Thee.

## Psalm XXXIV.

ord evermore will I give thanks to Thee,
And in my mouth Thy praise shall ever be;
My soul shall boast that she Thy servant is,
The humble shall be glad to hear of this;
Come then, O come, and let us praise the Lord,
And magnify His name with sweet accord.
I sought the Lord by prayer which He did hear,
And saved me from that ill my soul did fear.
Look towards God, thou shalt enlightenèd be,
And no foul shame shall ever light on thee.
The poor man's cry, the Lord doth quickly hear,
And doth for all his troubles quit him clear;
Such as fear God His Angel guards them all,
From every mischief that may them befall.
O taste the Lord, and see how sweet He is,
The man that trusts in Him lives still in bliss.
O fear the Lord, ye that are Saints of His,
Who fear the Lord no needful thing shall miss.
Rich become poor, and lions hungry be,
But such as fear the Lord no want shall see.
Come then ye children, listen and give ear,
And I will teach you this religious fear:
What man art thou that longest long to live,

And wouldst that God to thee good days should give;
Refrain thy tongue from speaking ill the while,
And from thy lips let there proceed no guile;
Do that is good, decline from that is ill,
Seek peace with God and men, and hold it still.
Upon good men God casts a gentle eye,
And bends a gentle ear unto their cry.
But to the wicked shows an angry brow,
Till they be quite exterpèd[8] root and bow;
But when the righteous cry, the Lord doth hear them
And from all troubles absolutely clear them;
God's present help the Lord's own folk doth find,
And such He saves as are of humble mind.
The righteous into many troubles fall,
But God's sweet mercy brings them out of all;
Their very bones so keep and count doth He,
As not one broken nor one lost shall be.
But some foul death shall on the wicked light,
And they which hate the just, shall perish quite;
But of his servants, God the Savior is;
They trust in Him, their hope they cannot miss.

## Psalm XXXV.

 lead Thou my cause, O Lord my Advocate!
Against all those with whom I have debate;
Fight against them that do against me fight,
Take up Thy shield, and help me with Thy might;
Lift up Thy lance, stop them which me pursue,
Say to my soul, I am Thy Savior true;
Let shame on them which seek my ruin light,
And with confusion turn them all to flight.
Let them be like the dust before the wind,
With God's fierce angel following them behind;
Set them in slippery ways, and dark withal,
And let God's Angel smite them as they fall;
For they have spread a net and dig'd a pit,

8   Cut off

Even without cause to catch my soul in it:
But in that pit let them fall unawares,
And be entangled in their proper snares;
But thou my soul, whom God thus guides from ill,
Rejoice in Him, and His salvation still;
My bones shall say, Lord who is like to Thee?
Who poor weak men from their strong foe dost free:
False witnesses arose with oaths untrue,
And chargèd me with things I never knew;
They to my grief did ill for good requite,
And recompensed my kindness with despite;
Yet in their sickness I did sackcloth wear,
And fast and pray with many a secret tear;
I could not more for friend or brother mourn,
Or if my mother to her grave were borne:
But in my woe they made great mirth and glee,
The very abject mocked and mowde[9] at me;
Base flatterers and jesters came withal,
And gnashed their teeth to show their bitter gall.
How long shall this be Lord? my soul withdraw
From these men's wrongs, and from the lion's jaw:
So in Thy Church shall I my thanks proclaim,
And in our Great Assembly praise Thy name;
Let not my foes triumph on me again,
Nor with their mocking eyes show their disdain;
They meet and part, but peace they do not seek
But to supplant the peaceable and meek;
They gape and draw their mouths in scornful wise,
And cry, fie, fie, we saw it with our eyes.
But Thou their deed (O Lord!) dost also see;
Then be not silent so, nor far from me.
Awake, stand up O God and LORD of Might,
Avenge my quarrel, judge my cause aright;
To Thy Doom rather let me fall or stand
Then subject be to their insulting hand;
Then they should say, so, so, these things go right,
We have our will, and have devoured him quite.
Shame be to them that joy in my mischance,

---

9  To wry the mouth, grimmace

And which to cast me down themselves advance;
Let them be glad that my well-wishers be,
And bless the Lord that hath so blessèd me.
As for my tongue it shall set forth Thy praise,
And celebrate Thy justice all my days.

## Psalm XXXVI.

he wicked man's bold sins my heart do tell,
No fear of God before his eyes doth dwell;
Yet flattereth he himself in his own sight,
Until his hateful deeds be brought to light;
His words are lies, and most deceitful too,
He leaves off quite all honest deeds to do;
He on his bed doth nought but mischief muse,
He shuns no ill and no good way doth choose;
Thy mercy Lord doth to the heavens extend,
Thy faithfulness doth to the Clouds ascend;
Thy justice steadfast as a Mountain is,
Thy Judgments deep as is the great Abyss;
Thy noble mercies save all living things,
The sons of men creep underneath Thy wings:
With Thy great plenty they are fed at will,
And of Thy pleasure's stream they drink their fill;
For even the well of life remains with Thee,
And in Thy glorious light we light shall see;
To them that know Thee, Lord, be loving still,
And just to them whose heart intends no ill;
Let not the foot of pride tread on my Crown
Nor the hand of the ungodly cast me down:
False are the wicked in their slippery ways,
And have no power again themselves to raise.

### Psalm XXXVII.

f ill men prosper do not Thou repine,
Nor envy them though they in glory shine;
For as the grass they shall be mown away,
And as green herbs shall turn to withered hay:
Trust thou in God and still be doing good,
And thou shalt never want no house nor food;
Delight in Him, He shall to thee impart,
The full desires and wishes of Thy heart;
On Him rely, to Him thy way commend,
And He shall bring it to a blessed end;
Thine upright light shall shine like the morning light;
And Thy just dealing like the Noonday bright;
Be still and fret not, but God's leisure stay
Though wicked men do prosper in their way;
Suppress Thine anger, let offenses die,
Lest thou be movèd to offend thereby;
Expect a while, observe what will befall;
Th' ungodly shall be gone, their place and all.
The Lord shall root out sinners out of hand,
When good men and their heirs shall hold their Land.
Meek persons shall enjoy the earth's increase,
And shall abound in plenty and in peace;
Against the just the wicked have combined,
And in despite their teeth at them they grind;
But God with scorn beholds them from the sky,
For that He sees their day of ruin nigh;
The ungodly draws his sword and bends his bow
To slay the just, the weak to overthrow:
But his bent bow shall break and make him start,
And his own sword shall pierce his wicked heart;
That little which the just enioys with peace,
'Tis better than th' ungodly's great increase;
For th' arms of impious men the LORD will break,
And give the righteous strength when they are weak;
The just man's days the LORD doth know and see,
That his inheritance shall endless be;
The times of danger shall not him confound,

And in the days of dearth, he shall abound;
Thy foes O Lord, shall perish and consume
Like fat of lambs, and vanish into fume;
Th' ungodly want and borrow, but repay not
The good men frankly give, and yet decay not;
Their seat is firm whom God hath best belov'd
But such as He doth curse shall be removed.
The good man's goings so directeth He
As it most pleasing to Himself may be;
Oft falls the just, yet is not cast away,
For God's own hand is his support and stay;
Though I am old, the just man or his seed
I never saw forsaken or in need;
He doth give daily alms, and frankly lend,
Which makes his offspring blessèd in the end;
Shun to do ill, be ever doing well,
And evermore thou shalt in safety dwell;
The LORD who loveth right, forsaketh never,
Those that are His, but keepeth them for ever;
His children He correcteth now and then,
But roots out quite the race of wicked men.
As long as Heaven shall move and Earth shall stand,
The righteous men inherit shall the Land;
The just man's mouth is wisdom's flowing well,
His tongue, of truth and judgement loves to tell;
And in his heart the law of God doth bide,
Which makes him walk upright and never slide;
The wicked sees the just with envious eye,
And lies in wait to wound him mortally;
But God will never leave him to his hands,
Nor him condemn when he in judgement stands:
Then wait thou on the Lord, and keep His way,
He shall thy patience with promotion pay;
Thy dwelling in the Land shall 'stablished be,
When thou the fall shalt of the wicked see.
The ungodly in great power myself have seen,
So that he flourished like a bay-tree green;
But soon as I passed by, and gone was he,
His place I sought, but no where could it see;

Keep a clear conscience, right and truth intend,
For that brings peace and comfort in the end;
When sinners shall at once together fall,
And in the end shall be exterpèd all;
But good mens' safety doth from God proceed,
Who is their strength in trouble, help at need;
Against the wicked He assists the just,
And rescues them, because in Him they trust.

## Psalm XXXVIII.

 f for my sins Thine anger kindled be,
Lord! let not then Thy justice chastise me;
Thine arrows fixèd in my flesh do stand,
I feel the pressure of Thy heavy hand;
I have no health Thine anger is so much,
My bones no rest; my grievous sin is such,
My wickedness doth mount above my head
And falling press me like a load of lead;
My ulcers are corrupted and do smell,
Caused by my folly, which I blush to tell.
I am with grief so broken and so torn,
As I all day in heart and habit mourn.
My loins are fillèd with a sore disease,
No part of all my body feeleth ease;
I am so faint, so feeble, and so sore,
As pain and anguish make me cry and roar;
Thou Lord! the longings of my heart dost see,
My sighs and groanings are not hid from Thee.
My heart doth pant, my sinews fail me quite,
My weeping eyes have lost their power of sight;
Meanwhile, my friends and neighbors they look on,
My nearest kinsmen farthest off are gone:
And they which seek my life have laid their snares
And set their traps, to catch me unawares.
They that to do me mischief lie in wait,
Do plot and practice nothing but deceit;
But as for me in silent patience
I seemèd deaf and dumb and void of sense;

As one whose ear admits not any sound,
And in whose mouth there is no answer found.
For on the Lord I evermore rely,
Though I stand mute, Thou shalt for me reply:
My suite is that my foes may not prevail
Who greatly joy to see my footing fail;
For in a place of stumbling set am I,
My sad estate is still before mine eye;
But I with sorrow will confess my sin,
And grieve that I offend my God therein;
And yet my foes do live and grow in might,
They grow in numbers which do bear me spite.
They which do ill for good, do hate me too,
Because I love good turns for ill to do:
Lord leave me not nor from me far depart,
Save me with speed: for Thou my safety art.

## Psalm XXXIX.

 said I will be wary in my way;
Lest I offend in that my tongue should say,
I will my mouth as with a bridle hold,
While wicked men with envy me behold:
I dumb did stand and from all speech refrain,
Even from good words, which was to me a pain:
My heart was hot: while I such doubts did cast,
The fire brake out, and thus I spake at last:
'Lord of my life reveal to me the end,
The period show, to which my days do tend!'
My life is but the measure of a span,
Nought as to Thee, so vain a thing is man:
Who dreaming walks, and toils for wealth in vain,
And doth not know to whom it shall remain.
But what do I expect? what is my hope!
Of my desires Thou art the only scope.
Lord! from my sins Thine indignation turn
And make me not to wicked fools a scorn,
When Thou didst strike I silent was and dumb
Because I knew the blow from Thee did come.

Remove Thy hand, withdraw Thy plague from me
Wherewith my vital spirits consumèd be:
Thy plagues for sin doth like a moth consume
Man's beauty vain, which is nought else but fume.
Lord! hear my prayer, and listen to my cries,
Let not Thy gracious eye my tears despise:
For I am but Thy guest, and sojourn here,
On earth a pilgrim as my fathers were;
O spare a little, and my strength restore
Before I go from hence to come no more.

## Psalm XL.

ong on the Lord, I waited patiently,
Till He inclined His ear, and heard my cry:
Drew me from out the pit of mire and clay
Did set me on firm ground and guide my way:
Put in my mouth a new and joyful song
Of thanks and praise, that to Himself belong.
Of His great mercy, many shall have sense,
And of the Lord have fear and confidence.
Blest is the man who hath on God relied,
Not turning unto lies or worldly pride;
O Lord! Thy works of wonder, they are such
Thy care and love to usward is so much,
They are so great, they are so numberless,
As if I would, I could not them express.
My sacrifice of meats Thou would'st not take,
But Thou mine ear didst pierce and open make.
Thou didst not ask burnt-offerings at my hand
Then, LORD, said I, 'I come at Thy command;
Thy Booke eternal, doth of me record,
That I should come to do Thy will O Lord!
To do Thy will, my heart is pleasèd well,
For in my heart Thy law doth ever dwell.'
Thy truth I have to all Thy people told,
Therein Thou knowest my tongue I cannot hold:
Thy justice in my heart is not conceal'd,
Thy mercy to the world I have revealed;

I have not spar'd to make Thy bounty known,
But in the Great Assembly have it shown.
Take not Thy wonted mercy Lord, from me,
But let Thy goodness still my safety be.
My troubles numberless such hold have took
On my weak soul, as up I cannot look:
My sins being more than hairs upon my head,
Make my heart faint and vital spirits dead:
But be it Lord, Thy pleasure and Thy will,
With speed to save and rescue me from ill:
Bring them to shame that would my life destroy,
Reprove them Lord, that wish my soul's annoy:
Let them be left to scorn and pride, which blame,
Which scorning say to me, fie, fie, for shame.
But let all those that seek their bliss in Thee,
Rejoice and say, 'The Lord's name praisèd be'.
For me who am contemptible and poor,
The Lord takes care, and feeds me evermore:
Thou Lord art my protection, and my aid,
Let not Thy gracious help be long delay'd.

## Psalm XLI.

hat man is blest who doth the poor regard;
In times of trouble God shall him reward,
Prolong his life, and bless him in the Land,
And free him from his foes' oppressing hand:
Shall comfort him, when sick and weak he lies,
And make his bed till he in health do rise:
My sin hath given my soul a grievous wound,
Apply Thy mercy Lord, and make it sound;
Thus speaks my foe of me to show his spite,
'When shall his life and honor perish quite?'
He visits me, but with false heart and tongue
And thereof vaunts, his 'complices among:
Even all my foes against me do conspire,
And with one mind my ruin do desire;
'Let him,' say they of me, 'in judgement fall
And when he once is down not rise at all.'

The friend I trusted, which did eat my bread,
Hath lifted up his heel against my head.
Thy mercy's wings on me O Lord display;
Raise me again, and I shall them repay.
By this I do Thy gracious favor see,
In that my foe doth not triumph on me.
Thou in my health upholds me with Thy hand,
And in Thy presence I shall ever stand.
The name of Jacob's God be blessèd then,
From age to age for evermore: Amen.

## Psalm XLII.

 s for the streams the hunted hart doth bray,
So for God's grace my heart doth pant and pray.
My soul doth thirst (O God of life!) for Thee,
When shall I come Thy blessed face to see?
My tears are all my food both night and day,
While 'where is now thy God?' the wicked say.
I pourèd out my heart, while thus I thought
And to God's House the multitude I brought:
With songs of praise and thankfulness withal,
To celebrate the Lord's great festival:
Then why art thou my soul so full of woe,
Unquiet in thyself and vexèd so?
O put thy trust in God and thankful be,
For his sweet help His presence yields to Thee.
My soul is grieved rememb'ring all the ill
I felt in Jordan's vale and Hermon hill.
One depth of sorrow doth to another call,
Thy waves O God have overgone me all:
I praised at night God's bounty of the day,
And unto Him that gives me life did pray.
God of my strength, why hast Thou left me so,
With heavy heart oppressèd by my foe?
My foe doth cut my bones as with a sword,
While he in scorn repeats this bitter word,
'Where is thy God?' his speech to me is such:
'Where is thy God, of which thou talked so much?'

But why art thou my soul dejected so?
Why art thou troubled and so full of woe?
Trust thou in God, and give Him thankful praise
Who is Thy present help in all thy ways.

## Psalm XLIII.

udge thou my cause, O God! and right me then,
Against ungodly and deceitful men.
O God, my strength, why set Thou me aside
And leave me to my foes' oppressing pride?
Send forth Thy light and truth and guide me still,
In the right way to Thy most holy hill.
God of my joy, before Thine Alter high,
My thankful heart, my harp shall justify.
Then why art thou my soul dejected so?
Why art thou troubled and so full of woe?
O put thy trust in God and thankful be,
For that sweet aide His presence gives to thee.

## Psalm XLIV.

ord! of Thy works, our fathers have us told,
Some in their days, and former times of old;
How Thou hast rooted out the Pagan race,
And Thy choice people planted in their place:
Who did not with their own sword win the Land,
Nor make the conquest with their proper hand;
But by Thine Arm, Thy favor, and Thy grace,
Thy countenance and brightness of Thy face;
Thou art my King, O God, and royal Guide,
And Thou for Jacob's safety dost provide.
We through Thine aid our foes do boldly meet,
And by Thy virtue cast them at our feet;
Therefore my trust I place not in my bow,
Nor in my sword, to save me from my foe.
Thou only saves us from our enemies,
Confounding them that do against us rise.

We boast and glory in our strength therefore,
And to Thy name sing praises evermore;
But now Thou standest off and leaves us quite,
And dost not lead our armies out to fight;
Thou makes us fly before our foes with fear,
While they from us rich spoils away do bear;
Like sheep, to feed them Thy poor flock is given,
Or scatterèd into several Nations driven.
Thine own dear people Thou dost sell for nought,
And sets on them no price when they are bought;
Thou hast us made unto our Neighbors all,
An object of reproach and scorn withal:
To Nations which do worship Idols dumb,
We are a byword of contempt become;
All the day long my shame is in my sight,
Which makes me hide my face and shun the light,
Not able to endure the blasphemies
And scorns of my revengeful enemies.
For all these ills we do not Thee forget,
Thy blessed Covenant we renounce not yet.
Our hearts recede not from the Law divine,
Nor do our footsteps from Thy paths decline;
Though we in dens of dragons have been placed,
And with death's fearful shadows overcast.
If we the name of our true God forget,
And Idols false we in His place do set,
Shall not He search it out, Whose eye doth see
The heart of man whose thoughts most troubled be?
But for Thy cause, LORD, we are martyred still,
Like sheep which Slaughter-Men cull out to kill.
Up Lord! why dost Thou seem to slumber thus?
Awake and be not always far from us:
Why hidest Thou from us Thy blessèd face,
Forgetting our distress and wretched case?
Our souls even to the dust are humbled low,
Our prostrate bodies to the ground do grow.
Arise and help us Lord! defend us still,
And save us for Thy mercy's sake from ill.

## Psalm XLV.

y heart is moved to utter some good thing,
Which I intend to offer to the king.
My tongue shall be the pen, and swiftly write
What in my heart devotion doth indite.
Fairest of men, whose lips with grace abound,
Whom with eternal blessings God hath crown'd;
Gird Thy sharp sword upon Thine armèd thigh,
And show Thyself in power and Majesty.
Ride on with Thy great honor prosperously,
Reign and triumph, and be Thou mounted high,
Borne up with justice, truth and meekness' wings:
And Thy right hand shall teach Thee dreadful things;
Thine arrows sharp, shall make Thy foes to fall,
Which Thou shalt shoot and pierce their hearts withal.
Eternal is Thy judgement-seat, O God!
Thy scepter is a true directing rod;
Right hast Thou loved and loathed unrighteousness,
And therefore God Thy God Who doth Thee bless,
Hath pour'd on Thee, O Prince of princes best,
More oil of gladness then on all the rest:
Thy garments, which Thy person shall array,
Brought out of Ivory wardrobes where they lay,
Of Myrrh, of Aloes, and of Casha smell;
Which odors do refresh and please Thee well.
The queen, all clad in gold at Thy right hand,
Daughters of Kings attending her, shall stand.
Attend fair daughter, listen and give ear,
Forget thy father's house and Country dear.
So shall the King take pleasure in thy beautie;
He is thy Lord, yield Him both love and duty.
The Tyrian virgins shall bring gifts to thee,
And Merchants rich, thy suppliants shall be.
The daughter of the King is rich without,
Her gowns embroidered all with gold about;
And yet within, she is more glorious far,
The jewels of her mind more precious are.
In finest dressing, with the needle wrought,

She with her fellow virgins shall be brought.
They shall with joy, O King be brought to Thee,
And in Thy princely Court receivèd be.
Thou in thy father's stead, O Bride shall gain
Sons, which in sundry Provinces shall reign.
Thee Lord, will I remember, all my days,
And all the world shall give Thee endless praise.

## Psalm XLVI.

OD is our hope and strength, which never fails;
Our present help, when mischief us assails.
Though the earth removèd, and the mountains were
Amid the Ocean cast, we would not fear.
Though raging seas a dreadful noise do make,
Though floods and tempests roaring, hills do shake,
There is a stream, which though it be not great,
Makes glad God's City, and His holy seat.
God in her Center dwells, and makes His place
Unmovable, by His preventing grace.
They were enraged which heathen kingdoms sway,
But when God spake, the Earth did melt away.
The Lord of Hosts assists us with His power,
And Jacob's God to us becomes a Tower.
Come, and behold what works the Lord hath wrought,
And He, His foes hath to destruction brought.
In all the world He war to peace doth turn,
The bow and spear do break and chariots burn;
Be quiet then and still, and know that I
Am Lord of the world and God Most High:
The Lord of Hosts assists us with His power,
And Jacob's God to us becomes a Tower.

### Psalm XLVII.

lap hands, ye people, with applause rejoice,
Sing to the Lord with loud and cheerful voice;
His throne is high, His judgement breedeth fear,
On all the earth He doth the Scepter bear.
He makes much people our command obey,
And many Nations at our feet doth lay;
And hath for us a heritage in store,
Even Jacob's portion whom He loved before.
In glorious triumph God is mounted high,
The Lord with trumpet's sound ascends the Sky.
Sing, sing, unto our God, unto our King,
All praises due, even all due praises sing.
All Kingdoms of the earth to Him belong,
Sing wisely then, and understand your song.
In all the heathen He doth reign alone,
And sits in judgment in His holy throne.
And heathen princes which were severed far,
To Abraham's faithful seed now joinèd are.
And God, Whose highness doth the heavens transcend,
As with a buckler doth the earth defend.

### Psalm XLVIII.

reat is the Lord and highly to be praised,
In God's own City, Sion hill is raised;
The beauty and the joy of all the Land,
The great king's City on the North doth stand;
In his fair Palaces God's name is known,
Where He doth cherish and protect His own.
Though many kings against her gathered be,
They stand astonished her great strength to see.
As when a woman doth in travail fall,
A sudden fear and trembling takes them all;
And God shall break them though they be combined,
As ships are broken with an Eastern wind.
What we have heard, we see Thou dost fulfill,
Thou God of Hosts upholds Thy City still:

Amidst Thy Temple, Lord, we do attend
Till Thou to us Thy grace and favor send.
Great is Thy name, O God, Thy praise no less,
And Thy right hand is full of righteousness.
Rejoice, O Sion, and your joys renew,
Daughters of Judah, for His judgements true.
About the walls of Sion walk ye round,
And tell the towers wherewith that fort is crowned;
Observe her bulwarks and her turrets high,
And tell the same to your posterity.
This ever living God our God is He,
And shall our Guide, while we have living, be.

## Psalm XLIX.

ear this ye people, all ye people hear;
Listen to me and give attentive ear,
All ye that in the world residing be,
Both rich and poor, of high and low degree:
My mouth shall utter, and my heart devise,
Matters of greatest skill, profound and wise.
Mine ears to parables will I incline,
And sing unto my harp of things divine.
Then why should I in ill times fearful be,
When mischief at my heels doth follow me.
Howbeit, some do in their riches trust,
And glory in their wealth, which is but dust;
Yet none from death his brother's life can stay,
Nor unto God for Him a ransom pay.
For it cost more the soul of man to save,
Then all the wealth is worth, which worldlings have.
Nor may men hope to live on earth for ever,
Though long they last, ere soul and body sever.
That fools and wise men die alike they find,
And unto strangers leave their wealth behind.
Their houses yet they think shall ever stand,
They give their proper names unto their land;
Yet no man can in honor ever be,
But as the brute beast dies, even so does he.

This is their folly, this their stumbling ways;
And yet the children do their fathers' praise.
They are shut up in graves as sheep in fold,
And hungry Death feeds on their bodies cold,
The just shall rule them when the sun doth rise,
With them their pride and beauty buried lies;
But God shall from Death's power my soul deliver,
When He shall take it to Himself for ever.
Then let not fear and envy thee surprise,
When thou seest men in wealth and honor rise,
For to their graves they nought away shall bear,
Nor shall their glory wait upon them there;
Yet they themselves thought happy all their days,
For him who helps himself others will praise:
As his forefathers all are gone before,
So shall he die and see the light no more.
So man on honor little doth foresee,
But as brute beasts do perish, so dies he.

## Psalm L.

 he Lord, the God of Gods, the world doth call,
Even from the sun's uprising to his fall;
From out of Sion doth the Lord appear,
And shows the brightness of His beauty clear.
In triumph, not in silence come shall He,
His usher fire, His guard a storm shall be.
He by His summons heaven and earth will call,
That He may judge at once his creatures all.
To Me, saith He, let all My saints repair,
Which worship Me with sacrifice and prayer;
God's justice shall from heaven declarèd be,
For Who is judge of all the world but He?
Hark Israel! I am Thy God, give ear;
I will against thee speak and witness bear.
Not for the daily task of sacrifice,
Or that burnt-offerings shine not in Mine eyes:
I want them not, nor will I take at all,
Goat from thy fold or bullock from thy stall;

All beasts are Mine within the forest wide,
And cattle on a thousand hills beside;
I know all fowls which in the air do fly,
And see all beasts which in the field do lie.
If I were hungry would I beg of thee,
When all things in the world belong to Me?
Art thou O man, so simple as to think
That bulls' flesh is My meat, goats' blood My drink?

## Psalm LXVII.

how us Thy mercy, Lord, and grace divine:
Turn Thy bright face that it on us may shine,
That all the men on Earth enlightened so
Their own salvation and Thy ways may know.
O let Thy people praise Thy blessed name,
And let all tongues and nations do the same;
And let all mortal men rejoice in this,
That God's their judge, and just His judgment is.
O let Thy people praise Thy blessèd name,
And let all tongues and nations do the same:
Then shall the Earth bring forth a rich increase,
And God shall bless us with a fruitful peace.
Even God shall bless us and His holy fear,
Possess the hearts of all men everywhere.

## Psalm XCI.

ho under the Most High Himself doth hide,
In most assurèd safety shall abide.
Thou art, O Lord, my hope and my defense,
My God, in Thee is all my confidence.
He shall preserve thee from the hunter's snare,
And from the pestilent contagious air.
His wings shall both protect and cherish thee,
His faithful promise shall thy buckler be.
No terror of the night shall thee dismay,
Nor Satan's arrow flying in the day,
Nor mortal plague, which in the dark annoys,

Nor that ill angel which at noon destroys.
Thousands, ten thousands shall about thee fall,
Yet no such ill shall thee approach at all;
Yea with thine eyes thou shalt behold and see,
The just reward of such as impious be;
Thou art my hope, I will on Thee rely,
Thy tower of safety, Lord, is set so high.
No mischief, no mischance shall thee betide
No plague come near the place where Thou shalt bide.
The Lord His angels will Thy keepers make,
In all Thy righteous ways which thou shalt take;
They in their hands shall thee sustain and stay
That Thou shalt never stumble in thy way.
Upon the basilisk and adder's head,
Dragon and lion thou shalt safely tread.
Thy love to Me shall save thee from mischance,
Thy knowledge of My name shall thee advance.
I will him hear, and help him in His trouble;
I will protect him and his honor double.
With length of days, he satisfied shall be,
And he at last shall My salvation see.

## Psalm XCV.

ome let us heartily rejoice and sing
To God our mightie Savior, and our King;
Present the praise which doth to Him belong,
And show our gladness in a cheerful song;
For God our Lord, the greatest God is He,
And Monarch of all gods that worshiped be.
The Earth's round globe, He holdeth in His hand:
And th' highest mountains are at His command.
The sea is His, He hath it made of old,
And the dry land His blessed hands did mold:
Come let us worship then, and humble fall
Before our mighty God which made us all.
He is our Lord, and we His people be;
Our shepherd, and His proper sheep are we.
This day if you His holy voice will hear,

Let not your hearts be hardened as they were,
When in the desert you His wrath did move,
And tempting Him His mighty power did prove.
Full forty years this nation grieved me so,
Their erring hearts My ways would never know;
Therefore displeased by oath I did protest
They never should possess my Land of rest.

## Psalm C.

e joyful in the Lord, ye nations all,
Cheer up your hearts in mirth, and songs withal;
The Lord is God, not we but He alone
Hath made us all, and feeds us every one.
Then enter ye His gates and courts with praise,
And strive with heart and voice His name to raise.
For why? the Lord is sweet, His mercy rare,
His truth for ever constant shall endure.

## Psalm CIII.

y soul with all thy powers thy Maker praise;
Forget not all His benefits to thee,
Who pardons all thy sins, and doth thee raise
When thou art fall'n through any infirmity:
Who doth thee save from mischiefs that would kill thee,
And crowneth thee with mercies ever more.
And with the best of things doth feed and fill thee,
And eagle-like thy youth and strength restore.
When men oppressèd do to Him appeal,
He righteth every one against his foe;
He unto Moses did His laws reveal,
And unto Jacob's ear His works did show.
He is more full of grace than we of sin;
To anger slow, compassionate, and kind;
He doth not ever chide, and never linne,[10]
Nor keeps displeasure always in His mind,

10  Cease

157

Nor after our misdeeds doth He us charge;
Nor takes He of our faults a strict account,
But as the space from earth to heaven is large,
So far His mercy doth our sins surmount.
As east from west is distant far away,
So far doth He from us our sins remove:
As fathers, kindness to their sons bewray,
So God to them that fear Him, shows His love.
For He that made us and knows all, doth know
The matter whereof man was made of old;
That we were formèd here on earth below
Of dust and clay, and of no better mold.
Man's age doth wither as the fading grass;
He flourisheth, but as ye flower in May,
Which when the South-wind over it doth pass
Is gone; and where it grew no man can say.
But God's sweet kindness ever doth consist;
His truth, from age to age, continue shall,
To them that in His righteous laws persist,
And think upon them to perform them all.
Heaven is God's seat; there doth His glory dwell,
But over all, His empire doth extend;
Praise Him ye angels which in strength excel,
And His command do evermore attend.
Praise Him ye hosts of heaven which serve Him there,
Whose service with His pleasure doth accord;
And praise Him all His creatures everywhere;
And thou my soul for thy part, praise the Lord.

## Psalm CL.

 o Him with trumpets and with flutes,
With cornets, clarions and with lutes;
With harps, with organs and with shawmes,[11]
With holy anthems and with psalms;
With voice of angels and of men
Sing! Alleluia! Amen, Amen.

---

11   Double-reed woodwind

# Miscellaneous Poems<sup>1</sup>

### A Hymn in Praise of Music

raise, pleasure, profit, is that threefold band,
Which ties men's minds more fast than Gordion's knots:
Each one some draws, all three none can withstand,
Of force conjoined, Conquest is hardly got.
Then Music may of hearts a Monarch be,
Wherein praise, pleasure, profit so agree.

Praise-worthy Music is, for God it praiseth,
And pleasant, for brute beasts therein delight,
Great profit from it flows, for why it raiseth
The mind overwhelmed with rude passions might:
    When against reason passions fond rebel,
    Music doth that confirm, and those expel.

If Music did not merit endless praise,
Would heavenly Spheres delight in silver round?
If joyous pleasure were not in sweet lays
Would they in Court and Country so abound?
    And profitable needs we must that call,
    Which pleasure linked with praise, doth bring to all.

Heroic minds with praises most incited,
Seek praise in Music and therein excel:
God, man, beasts, birds, with Music are delighted,
And pleasant t'is which pleaseth all so well:
    No greater profit is than self-content,
    And this will Music bring, and care prevent.

When antique Poets Music's praises tell,
They say it beasts did please, and stones did move:
To prove more dull than stones, then beasts more fell,
Those men which pleasing Music did not love;
    They fain'd, it Cities built, and States defended
    To show the profit great on it depended.

---

1  Unpublished in Davies' lifetime

Sweet birds (poor men's Musicians) never slake
To sing sweet Musics praises day and night:
The dying Swans in Music pleasure take,
To show that it the dying can delight:
    In sickness, health, peace, war, we do it need,
    Which proves sweet Music's profit doth exceed.

But I by niggard praising, do dispraise
Praise-worthy Music in my worthless Rime:
Ne can the pleasing profit of sweet lays,
Any save learnèd Muses well define:
    Yet all by these rude lines may clearly see,
    Praise, pleasure, profit in sweet music be.

## Ten Sonnets to Philomel

### Upon Love's ent'ring by the ears.

 ft did I hear our eyes the passage were,
By which Love entered to assail our hearts:
Therefore I guarded them, and void of fear,
Neglected the defense of other parts.
Love knowing this, the usual way forsook:
And seeking found a by-way by mine ear.
At which he ent'ring, my heart prisoner took,
And unto thee sweet Phylomel did bear.
Yet let my heart thy heart to pity move,
Whose pain is great, although small fault appear.
First it lies bound in fett'ring chains of love,
Then each day it is racked with hope and fear.
And with loves flames tis evermore consumed,
Only because to love thee it presumed.

O why did Fame my heart to love betray,
By telling my Dear's virtue and perfection?
Why did my Traitor ears to it convey
That Siren-song, cause of my heart's infection?
Had I been deaf, or Fame her gifts concealed,
Then had my heart been free from hopeless Love:

Or were my state likewise by it revealed,
Well might it Philomel to pity move.
Then should she know how love doth make me languish,
Distracting me twixt hope and dreadful fear:
Then should she know my care, my plaints and anguish,
All which for her dear self I meekly bear.
Yea I could quietly death's pains abide,
So that she knew that for her sake I died.

*Of his own, and his Mistress' sickness at one time.*

Sickness intending my love to betray,
Before I should sight of my dear obtain:
Did his pale colors in my face display,
Lest that my favor might her favors gain.
Yet not content herewith, like means it wrought,
My Philomel's bright beauty to deface:
And nature's glory to disgrace it sought,
That my conceivèd love it might displace.
But my firm love could this assault well bear,
Which virtue had, not beauty for his ground.
And yet bright beams of beauty did appear,
Through sickness veil, which made my love abound;
If sick (thought I) her beauty so excel,
How matchless would it be if she were well.

*Another of her sickness and recovery.*

Pale Death himself did love my Philomel,
When he her virtues and rare beauty saw,
Therefore he sickness sent: which should expel
His rival's life, and my dear to him draw.
But her bright beauty dazzled so his eyes,
That his dart life did miss, though her it hit:
Yet not therewith content, new means he tries,
To bring her unto Death, and make life flit.
But Nature soon perceiving, that he meant
To spoil her onely Phoenix, her chief pride,
Assembled all her force, and did prevent
The greatest mischief that could her betide.

So both our lives and loves, Nature defended:
For had she died, my love and life had ended.

*Allusion to Theseus' voyage to Crete, against the Minotaur.*

My love is sail'd against dislike to fight,
Which like vile monster, threatens his decay:
The ship is hope, which by desire's great might,
Is swiftly borne towards the wishèd bay:
The company which with my love doth fare,
(Though met in one) is a dissenting crew:
They are joy, grief, and never-sleeping care,
And doubt, which ne'er believes good news for true:
Black fear the flag is, which my ship doth bear,
Which (Dear) take down, if my love victor be:
And let white comfort in his place appear.
When love victoriously returns to me:
Lest I from rock despair come tumbling down,
And in a sea of tears be forced to drown.

*Upon her looking secretly out at a window as he passed by.*

Once did my Philomel reflect on me,
Her Christall pointed eyes as I passed by;
Thinking not to be seen, yet would me see:
But soon my hungry eyes their food did spy.
Alas, my dear, couldst them suppose, that face
Which needs not envy Phoebus chiefest pride,
Could secret be, although in secret place,
And that transparent glass such beams could hide?
But if I had been blind, yet Love's hot flame,
Kindled in my poor heart by thy bright eye,
Did plainly show when it so near thee came,
By more the usual heat than cause was nigh,
So though thou hidden wert, my heart and eye
Did turn to thee by mutual Sympathy.

When time nor place would let me often view
Nature's chief Mirror, and my sole delight;
Her lively picture in my heart I drew,

That I might it behold both day and night;
But she, like Philip's Son, scorning that I
Should portraiture, which wanted Apelles'[2] Art,
Commanded Love (who nought dare her deny)
To burn the picture which was in my heart.
The more love burn'd, the more her Picture shin'd:
The more it shin'd, the more my heart did burn:
So what to hurt her Picture was assign'd,
To my heart's ruin and decay did turn.
Love could not burn the Spirit, it was divine,
And therefore fir'd my heart, the Saint's poor shrine.

### To the Sun of his Mistress' beauty eclipsed with frowns.

When as the Sun eclipsèd is, some say
It thunder, lightning, rain, and wind portendeth;
And not unlike but such things happen may,
Since like effects my Sun eclipsèd sendeth!
Witness my throat made hoarse with thund'ring cries,
And heart with love's hot flashing lightnings fired:
Witness the showers which still fall from mine eyes,
And breast with sighs like stormy winds near rived.[3]
O shine then once again sweet Sun on me,
And with thy beams dissolve clouds of despair,
Whereof these raging Meteors framèd be,
In my poor heart by absence of my fair.
So shalt thou prove thy beams, thy heat, thy light,
To match the Sun in glory, grace, and might.

### Upon sending her a gold ring with this Posy.

Pure and Endless.

If you would know the love which I you bear,
Compare it to the Ring which your fair hand
Shall make more precious, when you shall it wear:
So my love's nature you shall understand.

---

2   Apelles of Kos, Greek painter from fourth century BC
3   Torn apart

Is it of metal pure? so you shall prove
My love, which ne're disloyal thought did stain.
Hath it no end? so endless is my love,
Unless you it destroy with your disdain.
Doth it the purer wax the more t'is tried?
So doth my love: yet herein they dissent,
That whereas gold the more t'is purified
By waxing less, doth show some part is spent:
My love doth wax more pure by your more trying,
And yet increaseth in the purifying.

### The heart's captivity.

My cruel dear having captiv'd my heart,
And bound it fast in chains of restless love:
Requires it out of bondage to depart,
Yet is she sure from her it cannot move.
Draw back (said she) your helpless love from me,
Your worth requires a far more worthy place:
Unto your suite though I cannot agree,
Full many will it lovingly embrace.
It may be so (my dear) but as the Sun,
When it appears doth make the stars to vanish!
So when yourself into my thoughts do run,
All others quite out of my heart you banish.
The beams of your perfections shine so bright,
That straight-way they dispel all other light.

### Of Fath the First Theological Virtue

aith is a sunbeam of th' Eternal light,
That in man's soul infused by grace doth shine:
Which gives her dazzled eye so clear a sight
As evidently sees the truth divine;
This beam that clears our eyes, inflames our hearts,
And Charity's kind fire doth there beget:
For sunlike, it both light and heat imparts:
Faith is the light, and Charity the heat:
This light of faith the noblest wisdom is,

For it the only truth allows and applies:
The virgin's lamp, that lights the soul to bliss;
The Jacob's scales, whereby she climbs the skies;
The eye that sees, the hand that apprehends;
The cause of causes, and the end of ends.

## A Song of Contention

*Between four maids concerning that which addeth most perfection
to that sex.*

### The First for Beauty.

ur fairest Garland, made of Beauty's flowers,
Doth of itself supply all other dowers:
Women excel the perfects[4] men in this,
And therefore herein their perfection is:
For beauty we the glorious heavens admire;
Fair fields, fair houses, gold and pearl, desire.
Beauty doth always health and youth employ
　　and doth delight the noblest sense, the eye.

### The Second for Wit.

Beauty delights the soul, but wit the Reason:
Wit lasts an age, and beauty but a season:
The sense is quickly cloyed with beauty's taste;
When wit's delight still quick and fresh doth last:
Beauty, weak eyes with her illusion blinds,
Wit conquers spirits and triumphs over minds:
Dead things have beauty, only man hath wit,
　　and man's perfection doth consist in it.

### The Third for Wealth.

Wealth is a power that passeth nature far:
Makes every goose a swan, and spark a star:

---

4  Perfectest

Queen money brings and gives with royal hands
Friends, kindred, honor, husband, house, and lands;
Not a fair face, but fortune fair, I crave,
    Let me want wit so I fools' fortune have.

### The Fourth for Virtue.

Yet those perfections most imperfect be,
If there be wanting virtuous modesty;
Virtue's aspect would have the sweetest grace
If we could see as we conceive her face:
Virtue guides wit, with well-affected will,
Which if wit want, it proves a dangerous ill:
Virtue gains wealth with her good government,
    If not, she's rich, because she is content.

## A Maid's Hymn in Praise of Virginity

 acred virginity, unconquered Queen!
Whose kingdom never hath invaded been;
Of whose sweet rosy crown no hand hath power
    Once but to touch, much less to pluck a flower:

'Gainst whom proud Love—which on the world doth reign,—
With armies of his passions fights in vain;
In whom gray Winter never doth appear,
    To whom green Springtide lasteth all the year.

O fresh immortal bay, untroubled well,
Or violet, which untouched dost sweetest smell;
Fair vine, which without prop dost safely stand,
    Pure gold, new coined, which never passed a hand.

O temperance, in the supreme degree
And highest pitch that virtue's wings can flee:
O more than humane spirit, of Angels' kind:
    O white, unspotted garment of the mind,

Which first clothed man, before he was forlorn;
And wherein God Himself chose to be born.

Within my soul, O heavenly virtue rest,
  Until my soul with heaven itself be blest.


## Part of an Elegie in Praise of Marriage

hen the first man from Paradise was driven,
  He did from thence his only comfort bear:
  He still enjoys his wife, which God had given,
    Though he from other joys divorcèd were.

This cordial comfort of society,
This truelove knot, that ties the heart and will,
When man was in th' extremest misery
  To keep his heart from breaking, existed still.

There is a tale then when the world began,
Both sexes in one body did remain:
Till Jove, offended with that double man,
  Caused Vulcan to divide him into twain.

In this division, he the heart did sever,
But cunningly he did indent the heart,
That if they should be reunited ever,
  Each part might know which was the counterpart:

Since when, all men and women think it long,
Each of them their other part have met:
Sometimes they meet ye right, sometimes ye wrong,
  This discontent, and that doth joy beget.

It joy begets in their indented hearts,
When like indentures they are matched aright:
Each part to other mutual joy imparts,
  And thus the man which Vulcan did divide,

Is now again by Hymen made entire,
And all the ruin is reedified;[5]
Two being made one by their divine desire.
  Sweet marriage is the honey never cloying;

---

5   Rebuilt

The tune, which being still played, doth ever please,
The pleasure which is virtue's in enjoying.
It is the band of peace and yoke of ease,
    It is a yoke, but sweet and light it is;

The fellowship doth take away the trouble,
For every grief is made half less by this,
And every joy is by reflection double.
    It is a band, but one of Love's sweet bands,

Such as he binds the world's great parts withal:
Whose wondrous frame by their convention stands,
But being disbanded would to ruin fall.

## A Fragment of a Love Elegy

ut those impressions by this form are stained,
and blotted out as if they had not been:
And yet if nothing else in mind I bear,
makes me not less learn[è]d than before:
For that in her as in a mirror clear,
I see and learn far better things and more.
The students of the world and Nature's book,
Beauty and order in the world do note;
She is my little world; on her I look,
and do in her the same perfections quote:
For in her eyes the beams of beauty shine,
and in her sweet behavior and her grace,
Order appears, and comeliness divine,
Befitting every time and every place.

3.

Unto that sparkling wit, that spirit of fire,
That pointed diamond look, that eagle's eye
Whose lightning makes audacity retire
and yet draws on respective modesty,
With wings of fear and love, my spirit doth fly
and doth therein a flame of fire resemble;
Which, when it burns most bright and mounts most high,

then doth it waver most and most doth tremble.
O that my thoughts were words, or could I speak
The tongue of Angels, to express my mind:
For mortal speech is far too faint and weak
to utter passion of so high a kind.
You have a beauty of such life and light
As it hath power all wand'ring eyes to stay:
To move dumb tongues to speak, lame hands to write,
Staid thoughts to run, hard hearts to melt away:
Yet painters can of this draw every line
And every witless person that hath eyes,
Can see and judge and swear it is divine:
For in these outward forms all fools are wise.
But that which my admiring spirit doth view,
In thought whereof it would for ever dwell,
Eye never saw, the pencil never drew,
Pen never could describe, tongue never tell:
It is the invisible beauty of your mind,
Your clear imagination, lively wit,
So tuned, so tempered, of such heavenly kind,
As all men's spirits are charmed and rapt with it.
This life within begets your lively look,
As fire doth make all metals look like fire;
Or your quick soul by choice this body took,
As angels with bright forms themselves attire.
O that my breast might ope, and heart might cleave
That so you might my silent wond'ring view:
O that you might my soaring spirit perceive,
How still with trembling wings it waits on you.
Then should you see of thoughts an endless chain,
Whose links are virtues, and your virtues be;
Then should you see how your fair form doth reign
Through all the regions of my fantasy.
Then should you find that I was yours as much
As are your sharp conceits borrowed of none;
Or as your native beauties, that are such
As all the world will swear it is your own.

## 4.

As they that work in mines, rich veins bewray,
By some few grains of ore whereon they hit:
And as one letter found is oft a kay
To many lines that are in cipher writ;
So I by your few loving lines descry
Of your long hidden love the golden mine;
And read therein with a true lover's eye
Of the heart's volume, every secret line.
But what avails it now, alas to know
That once a blessed man I might have been?
Since I have let, by looking down too low
My highest fortunes sore away unseen:
And yet if I had raised my humble eyes
As high as heaven I could not have discerned
Of invisible thoughts which in your heart did rise,
Unless of you I had my lesson learned.
But all was dark and folden up to me;
As soon might I myself, myself have taught
To read the black records of destiny,
As read the riddles of the silent thought:
But whereto may I best resemble this?
Your love was like the springing of a tree:
We cannot see the growing when it is,
But that it hath sprung up and grown, we see.
Or it is like to wealth by fairies brought,
Which they bring still while they invisible go;
But all doth vanish and doth turn to nought,
If once a man enriched, those fairies know:
But now your love (say you) is dead and gone:
But my strong faith shall give it life again.
By strength of fancy miracles are done,
And true belief doth seldom hope in vain.
Your Phoenix love is unto ashes turned,
But now the fire of my affection true,
Which long within my heart hath kindly burned,
Shall spread such heat as it shall live anew.
Or if the fire of your celestial love,
Be mounted up to heaven and cannot die:

Another sly Prometheus will I prove,
and play the thief to steal it from the sky.
When you vouchsafed to love unworthy me,
Your love descended like a shower of rain;
Which on the earth, even senseless though she be,
when once it falls, returneth not again.
Then why should you withdraw the heavenly dew
Which fell sometimes on your despairing lover?
Though then his earthly spirit full little knew
How good an Angel did about him hover.
O you the glory of your sex and race!
You that all times and places happy make!
You that in being virtuous virtue grace,
and make men love it better for your sake:
One sunbeam yet of favor cast on me,
Let one kind thought in your clear fancy rise:
Love but a thought, or if that may not be
Be pleased that I may love, it shall suffice.

## To the Q[ueen]

hat Music shall we make to you?
To whom the strings of all men's hearts
Make music of ten thousand parts:
In tune and measure true,
With strains and changes new.

How shall we frame a harmony
Worthy your ears, whose princely hands
Keep harmony in sundry lands:
Whose people divers be,
In station and degree?
    Heaven's tunes may only please,
    and not such airs as these.

For you which down from heaven are sent
Such peace upon the earth to bring,
Have heard the choir of Angels sing:
and all the spheres consent,
like a sweet instrument.

How then should these harsh tunes you hear
Created of ye troubled air,
breed but distaste—when you repair—
to your celestial ear?
So that this center here
for you no music finds,
but harmony of minds.

### [To Fair Laides]

adies of Founthill, I am come to seek
My heart amongst you, which I late did lease;
but many hearts may be perhaps alike:
Therefore of mine, the proper marks, are these.
It is not hard, though true as steel it be,
And like ye diamond, clear from any spot;
Transmixed with many darts you shall it see,
but all by virtue, not by Cupid, shot;
It hath no wings, because it needeth none,
Being now arrived and settled where it would;
Wingèd desires and hopes from it gone are,
but it is full of joys as it can hold.
Fain would I find it where it doth remain,
but would not have it though I might again.

### Upon a Pair of Garters

o loving wood-bind, clip with lovely grace,
those two sweet plants which bear ye flowers of love;
Go silken vines, those tender elms embrace,
Which flourish still, although their roots do move.
As soon as you possess your blessed places,
You are advancèd and ennobled more
Then diadems, which were white silken laces
That ancient kings about their forehead wore:
Sweet bands, take heed lest you ungently bind,
Or with your strictness make too deep a print:
Was never tree had such a tender rind,

Although her inward heart be hard as flint;
And let your knots be fast, and loose at will,
she must be free, though I stand bounden still.

## [To His Lady-Love]

n this sweet book, ye treasury of wit,
All virtues, beauties, passions, written be:
And with such life they are set forth in it
as still methinks that which I read I see.
But this book's Mrs. is a living book,
Which hath indeed those virtues in her mind,
And in whose face though envy's self do look,
Even envy's eye shall all those beauties find.
Only the passions that are printed here,
In her calm thoughts can no impression make:
She will not love, nor hate, nor hope, nor fear,
Though others seek these passions for her sake.
So in the sun, some say there is no heat
though his reflecting beams do fire beget.

## [Tobacco]

omer of Moly and Nepenthe sings:
Moly, the gods' most sovereign herb divine.
Nepenthe Hellen's drink, which gladness brings—
Heart's grief repels, and doth ye wits refine.
But this our age another world hath found,
From whence an herb of heavenly power is brought:
Moly is not so sovereign for a wound
Nor hath Nepenthe so great wonders wrought.
It is tobacco: whose sweet subtle fume
The hellish torment of the teeth doth ease,
By drawing down and drying up the rheum
The mother and the nurse of each disease.

## Elegies of Love

ike as the diverse-fretchled[6] Butterfly,
When Winter's frost is fall'n upon his wing,
Hath only left life's possibility,
    and lies half dead until the cheerful Spring:

But then the Sun from his all-quick'ning eye,
Darts forth a sparkle of the living fire:
Which with kind heat, doth warm the frozen fly
    and with new spirit his little breast inspire:

Then doth he lightly rise and spread his wings,
And with the beams that gave him life doth play:
Tastes every flower that on th' earth's bosom springs,
    and is in busy motion all the day:

So my gay Muse, which did my heart possess,
And in my youthful fantasy doth reign:
Which cleared my forehead with her cheerfulness
    and gave a lively warmth unto my brain:

With sadder study, and with grave conceit
Which late my Imagination entertained:
Began to shrink, and loose her active heat,
    and dead as in a lethargy remained.

Long in that senseless sleep congealed she lay,
Until even now another heavenly eye,
And clear as that which doth beget the day,
    and of a like reviving sympathy:

Did cast into my eyes a subtle beam,
Which piercing deep, into my fancy went,
And did awake my muse out of her dream,
    and unto her new life and virtue lent:

So that she now begins to raise her eyes
Which yet are dazzled with her beauty's ray;
And to record her wonted melodies,
    Although at first she be not full so gay.

---

6  Freckled

## The King's Welcome

 now or never gentle muse be gay,
And mount up higher on thy paper wings,
Than doth the lark when he salutes the day,
And to the morn a merry welcome sings.

Fly swifter than the eagle sent by art
From Nuremberg, to the Almaine emperor:
A hand less cunning, but as true a heart
Sends thee to a prince of greater worth and power.

Rencounter[7] him thou shalt upon the way,
like Phoebus midst of all his golden train;
And know him too thou shalt at first survey
By proper notes and by distinctions plain.

By his fair outward forms and princely port,
by honors done to him with cap and knee;
He is deciphered by the vulgar sort,
but truer characters will rise to thee.

Thy sight had once an influence divine.
which gave it power the soul of man to view;
wipe and make clean that dazzled eye of thine,
and thou shall see his real marks and true.

Look over all that divers troop, and find
who hath his spirits most Jovial and free,
whose body is best tempered, and whose mind
Is ever best in tune, and that is he.

See who it is whose actions do bewray
that threefold power, which rarely mixed we see;
A judgment grave, and yet a fancy gay,
Joined with a rich remembrance, that is he.

Mark who it is, that hath all noble skill,
which may to public good referrèd be;
the quickest wit, and best affected will,
whence flows a stream of virtues, that is he.

---

7 To meet by chance

If any more than other clearly wise
or wisely just or justly valiant be;
If any do faint pleasures more despise,
or be more master of himself, 'tis he

But soft, the Eaglet's eye will soon be dim
If thou this rising sun directly view;
look sideways on the beams that spread from him;
fair peace, rich plenty, and religion true.

Besides a guard of blessed angels hover
about his sacred person, day and night;
and with invisible wings his head do cover,
that danger's darts thereon may never light

When by these proper notes thou shalt him ken,
fly towards him with wings of love and fear;
like fire which most doth wane and tremble then
when it doth mount most high and burn most clear.

Yet on; for wingèd time with thee goes on,
which like old Æson hath his youth renewed;
his hourglass turnèd and his sickle gone,
and all his gray and broken feathers mewed.

On, for the brave young son above his head
Comes Northward, that he may his glory meet;
whilst the fresh earth in all her pride doth spread
green velvet carpets underneath his feet.

On, for the birds will help to fill thy song,
whereto all english heart strings do agree;
And the Irish harp strings, that did jar so long
to make the music full, now tunèd be.

There is no eye cast down, there is no voice
that to pronounce the heart assent, is dumb;
the world of things doth everywhere rejoice,
in certain hope of blessed times to come

Thousands while they possess and fill the ways
doth both desire, and hinder his repair;
they fill the empty heaven with prayer and praise,
which he requites with demonstrations faire.

Then what hast thou to do, and what remains?
pray as the people doth, and add but this,
This little wish; that whiles he lives and reigns,
he may be still the same, that now he is.

### To the Queen at the Same Time

f we in peace had not received the king
We see we had been conquered, since we see
The Queen such armies doth of beauties bring
    As all our eyes and hearts her vassals be.

The Danish armies once great honor won
Upon this Land; yet conquered but a part.
But you great Lady more, alone, have done;
    For at first sight you conquer'd every heart.

Star of the North! upon these Northern Realms
Long may your virtues and your beauties reign:
Beyond our Cynthia's years, whose golden Beams
    Are set with us, and cannot shine again:

Well may it be; though sun and moon go down
    Seas have no power the North pole star to drown.

### Verses Sent to the King with Figs

o add unto the first man's happiness,
His maker did for him a garden make;
And placed him there, that he the same might dress,
And pleasure great with little labour take.
    And this with nature stands, and reason right,
That man who first was formèd of the earth
In trimming of the earth should take delight,

And her adorn from whom he took his birth.
Nor her for this doth he ungrateful find;
For she in gardens her best fruits doth yield.
The Earth in gardens is a mother kind,
When she is but a step-dame in the field.
Sir, in your service God hath me so blest
As I have been enabled to acquire
A garden, ready planted, trimmed and dressed,
Whereto in vacant times I do retire.
This garden, and the fruit thereof, indeed
Are fruits of your great favor unto me;
And therefore all the fruits which thence proceed
A proper offering to your Highness be:
 But if this verse or boldness, merit blame,
 Those fig leaves, Sr. I hope shall hide the same.

# ROMAN ROADS CLASSICS

Also available from Roman Roads Press:

*The Iliad* and *The Odyssey* of Homer,
a new prose rendering by Wesley Callihan

*Paradise Lost & Paradise Regained* by John Milton

ROMAN ROADS CLASSICS

*Inferno: Book One of the Divine Comedy, Dante Alighieri,*
a blank verse translation by Joe Carlson

*Purgatorio: Book Two of the Divine Comedy, Dante Alighieri,*
a blank verse translation by Joe Carlson

*Paradiso: Book Three of the Divine Comedy, Dante Alighieri,*
a blank verse translation by Joe Carlson

*The Prose Works of Dante Alighieri, Volume I: The Italian Works*
Preface & Introduction by Joe Carlson

*The Prose Works of Dante Alighieri, Volume II: The Latin Works*
Preface & Introduction by Joe Carlson

Cicero's *On Duties*

# ON DUTIES

Marcus Tullius Cicero

Translated by Walter Miller
FOREWORD BY WESLEY J CALLIHAN